The Quilted Nursery

More Than 50 Coordinated Projects for Baby

Leslie Beck

Martingale
& COMPANY

Bothell, Washington

Credits

President . . . . Nancy J. Martin
CEO/Publisher . . . . Daniel J. Martin
Associate Publisher . . . . Jane Hamada
Editorial Director . . . . Mary V. Green
Design and Production Manager . . . . Cheryl Stevenson
Technical Editor . . . . Darra Williamson
Copy Editor . . . . Liz McGehee
Illustrators . . . . Laurel Strand, Patty Wagner
Photographer . . . . Brent Kane
Book design and composition . . . . Rohani Design

That Patchwork Place is an imprint of Martingale & Company.

MISSION STATEMENT

We are dedicated to providing quality products and service by working together to inspire creativity and to enrich the lives we touch.

The Quilted Nursery: More Than 50
Coordinated Projects for Baby
© 1999 by Leslie Beck

Martingale & Company
PO Box 118
Bothell, WA 98041-0118 USA
www.patchwork.com

Printed in Hong Kong
04 03 02 01 00 99   6 5 4 3 2 1

Dedication

To my husband, Byron, Sr., and my children, Byron, Jr., Christine, and Kate. They have always believed in me, supported me, and urged me forward. Without their love and patience I would not have been able to pursue my design career.

And, to quilters everywhere, it is my sincere hope that the *Quilted Nursery* collection will be today's joy and tomorrow's cherished memory.

Acknowledgments

The Quilted Nursery was brought to life with the help and dedication of my talented team:

Retta Warehime, quilt designer and author. She led my staff through many hours of measuring, cutting, sewing, writing, and editing.

Elisabeth Lafferty, Shirley Christensen, Debbie Baalman, Jerrine Kirsch, Gayla Winsor, Shawna Holland, Lera Beck, and Jayme Warehime, excellent piecers, quilters, and sewers.

Special recognition to Pat Wagner and Earlene Sullivan, Byron Beck and Kate Beck, for the computer graphics and text.

Credit for the Secret Garden floor cloth goes to Kathy Renzelman, a decorative painter.

Thanks to all for the team effort and commitment.

Library of Congress Cataloging-in-Publication Data

Beck, Leslie, 1946–
    The quilted nursery / Leslie Beck.
       p. cm.
     ISBN 1-56477-288-8
     1. Patchwork—Patterns. 2. Nurseries—Equipment and supplies. 3. House furnishing. 4. Machine sewing. 5. Applique—Patterns.
    I. Title.
    TT835.B427 1999
    746.46'041—dc21   99-44335
                                        CIP

Contents

Preface

The *Quilted Nursery* was inspired by today's trend toward a consistent decorative style throughout the home. The bed, bath, and living room often speak the same style, but frequently the nursery is overlooked.

I designed this collection using simple, "old favorite" pieced blocks, such as Pinwheel and Log Cabin, and appliqués that can be applied invisibly by hand or with lightweight fusible web and a decorative blanket stitch. Colors and styles range from a renewed century-old crib quilt, to the modern bright-and-bold look. Each collection includes a variety of theme-related accessories, such as a crib quilt, bumper pad, headboard, dust ruffle, window treatment, pillow, and wall hanging.

Have fun exploring all the possibilities, and create a "Quilted Nursery" just right for that special new little person.

Materials and Supplies

None of the projects in the Quilted Nursery collection require unique or hard-to-find materials, notions, or supplies. You'll probably find much of what you need—with the exception of fabric and batting—already in your sewing room.

Rotary cutter and mat: A large rotary cutter enables you to quickly cut the strips and pieces you'll need for most of these projects. A self-healing mat protects both the cutter blade and the tabletop.

Cutting guides: You'll need a ruler to measure fabric and to guide the rotary cutter. There are many appropriate rulers, but one of my favorites is the thick 24" acrylic plastic type that includes gridded lines for cutting strips, guidelines for marking and cutting 45° and 60° angles, and ¼" increments marked along the edge. A guide such as a Bias Square® is useful for squaring up blocks and for making certain that the ruler is properly positioned on the fabric for rotary cutting. Visit your local quilt shop to choose your own personal favorites from the many options available.

Sewing machine: You don't need anything fancy: just a reliable straight-stitch machine in good working order. Adjust the stitch length so the stitches hold seams in place securely, but are easy to remove if necessary. Of key importance is the ability to gauge an accurate ¼" seam allowance. If you do not have a ¼" foot for your machine, contact your machine dealer or local quilt shop for assistance, or mark your machine as suggested in "Machine Piecing" on page 8.

Thread: Use a good-quality, all-purpose, 100% cotton, cotton-wrapped polyester, or polyester sewing thread. Do not use prewaxed hand quilting thread in your sewing machine.

Pins: Keep a good supply of glass- or plastic-headed pins nearby. Long pins are especially helpful for pinning multiple thick layers together. A visit to your local quilt shop will help you decide which pins are best for your project.

Iron and ironing board: These are essential as you'll want to press frequently and carefully to ensure smooth, accurately stitched results. An experienced quilter may tell you that she spends more time pressing than sewing.

Needles: Use sewing-machine needles sized for cotton fabrics, such as 70/10 or 80/12. Keep a sharp needle in the machine. A dull needle inter-feres with tension and causes skipped, loose, or uneven stitches. In addition, keep an assortment of hand sewing and quilting needles available in sizes such as #8, #9, and #10.

> **Tip**
>
> A popping sound as the needle pierces the fabric is a good clue that it's time to change the needle on your sewing machine.

Fabric

While the most expensive fabric is not necessarily best, a good rule of thumb in selecting fabric is to buy the best you can afford. Light- to medium-weight 100% cotton fabric produces the best results in any quilting project. A good-quality cotton is reasonably wrinkle-free, uniform, and closely woven with long, fine threads. Avoid poor-quality fabric that wrinkles easily and is uneven or loosely woven with short, weak threads.

Color is a personal choice. The only person to please is you. If you are unsure how to select colors that will look nice together in a finished project, try the "blender technique." A blender fabric is one with four or more colors. Choose a bolt of fabric you really love and use this bolt as a palette to select additional fabrics. The fabric designer has already done the work of coordinating the colors for you! If you like the colors in the blender fabric and choose those colors for coordinating fabrics, chances are you will be pleased with the finished project.

Arrange your fabric choices on the background fabric you've chosen, then stand back. Take off your glasses, squint, or use a Ruby Beholder® value-finding tool to see if any fabrics blend too closely. For best results, include a good range of lights, mediums, and darks, and keep each value distinct. If any of the fabrics are too close in value, substitute another fabric until you have the right contrast.

View the scale of the prints in relation to how they will be used in the project. If you need just a small piece in the block, use a small-scale print. A large piece can more successfully showcase a large-scale print.

The fabric amounts listed for the individual projects assume that the fabric is at least 42" wide after laundering and pressing.

General Sewing Techniques

The following are some basic cutting, stitching, and embellishing guidelines to help you complete the projects in this book.

ROTARY CUTTING

The pieced projects in *The Quilted Nursery*'s various collections are Template-Free®. You'll rotary cut strips, then crosscut strips into smaller segments and combine them to complete the necessary blocks and units. All rotary measurements include ¼"-wide seam allowances, unless otherwise noted.

Note: Reverse the following rotary-cutting techniques if you are left-handed.

1. Fold fabric in half lengthwise, matching the selvages. Place the fabric on the cutting mat so that the length of fabric lies to your right, with the raw edges on the left.
2. Align a Bias Square ruler with the fold and place a long ruler against it. Remove the Bias Square and press firmly on the ruler to keep it from moving. Place the cutter blade next to the ruler and, exerting an even pressure on the rotary cutter, begin cutting. Always roll the cutter away from yourself! As you cut, move your fingers along the ruler as necessary to hold it steadily in place. After cutting, check to see if all the layers have been cut. If not, try again, this time applying more pressure to the cutter.
3. Keeping the fabric to your right, use the ruler to measure a strip of the appropriate width from the left straight edge. If, for instance, you need a 2½" × 42" strip of fabric, align the fabric edge with the 2½" line on the ruler and cut along the ruler's edge.

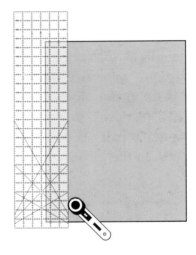

4. Turn the strip horizontally and cut to the desired shape and size.

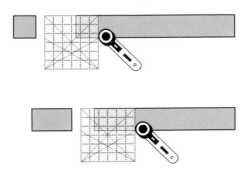

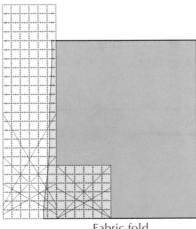

Fabric fold

MACHINE PIECING

Accuracy is important when machine piecing. Unless otherwise noted, use a ¼"-wide seam allowance for all the projects in this book. Move the needle position so that it is ¼" from the right side of the presser foot, or measure ¼" to the right of the needle and mark the seam allowance on the sewing machine with a piece of masking tape. For many of today's machines, you can also buy a presser foot that measures ¼" from the needle to the outside edge.

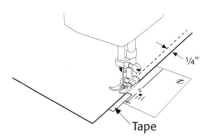

Tape

Often, you can save time and thread by chain piecing. Place pieces to be joined right sides together and pin as necessary. Stitch the seam, but do not lift the presser foot or cut the connecting threads; just feed in the next pair of pieces. Join as many pairs as possible, then clip the threads between the pieces.

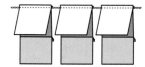

Matching Points

It is not always easy to line up seams and match points perfectly, especially if you rely on chance! Try these simple techniques to help achieve perfect points.

- Poke a pin into one point along the seam line and through to the seam or other point it must match. Slide the fabric pieces together until the pin is perpendicular to the fabric and the pieces line up. Pin securely on both sides of the point you are matching. Remove the first pin and stitch.

- Whenever possible, work with opposing seam allowances. When matching seam lines for sewing, make sure the seam allowance on the bottom layer is pressed so that it moves easily over the feed dogs, then press the top seam allowance in the opposite direction. This "locks" the seams into position so you can line them up exactly. Pin the seam allowances in place if necessary.

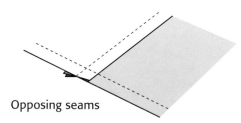

Opposing seams

- If the pieces being joined are slightly different in length, pin the pieces together at the ends and at the seam, then sew with the longer piece on the bottom, against the feed dogs. The feed dogs will ease the fullness on the bottom piece, coaxing both pieces through the needle together.

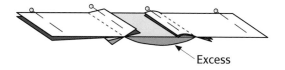

Excess

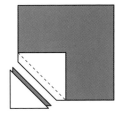
For extra-tricky junctions, stitch to 1" to ½" from the intersection and stop with the needle down. Set the sewing machine for longer stitches, then continue stitching ½" to 1" past the intersection. With the needle still down, return to the standard stitch length and resume stitching. When you finish the seam, check to see if the points match. If they do, simply re-stitch over the long stitches. If not, you can easily remove the long stitches, adjust, re-pin, then try again until the points match.

Angled Piecing

The following Template-Free methods of sewing angles are more accurate, less intimidating, and even easier than using templates! Choose your method based upon the direction of the angle or the number of angles in each piece.

When sewing angles, place the fabrics right sides together and draw a diagonal line on the wrong side of one of the pieces. Use a fine-point marker or sharp pencil to draw the line at the angle shown in the illustration. Sew exactly on the drawn line and cut away the excess fabric, leaving a ¼"-wide seam allowance.

To sew a small square to a larger piece:
1. Draw a diagonal line on the wrong side of the small square.
2. With right sides together, lay the square over the other fabric piece as indicated, making sure the diagonal line lies in the proper direction for your particular unit.

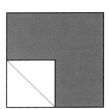

3. Stitch directly on the diagonal line and cut away the excess fabric, leaving a ¼"-wide seam allowance. Press the seam allowances

toward the dark fabric unless directed otherwise. When sewing two or more squares to another piece of fabric, add one square, cut away the excess, and press. Then add the next square, cut away, and press, repeating until you've added all the squares.

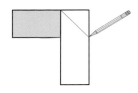

To sew a rectangle to a rectangle:
1. With right sides together, lay one rectangle on top of the other at a 90° angle, matching corners.

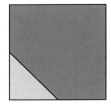

2. Draw a line at a 45° angle from the corner of the top rectangle to the corner of the bottom rectangle.

3. Stitch along the diagonal line and cut away the excess fabric, leaving a ¼"-wide seam allowance. Press seam allowances toward the darker fabric unless directed otherwise.

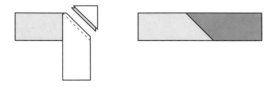

For a rectangle with an angled seam at each end, sew a rectangle to each end of the center rectangle, one at a time, then cut away the excess and press.

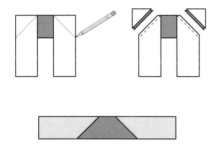

PRESSING

Place a freshly laundered, folded towel on the ironing board when pressing blocks. The towel helps ease out any unwanted fullness, so the project will lie flat.

Do not use steam. It can distort pieces (especially smaller ones) and even alter the block shape. Use a spray bottle with water instead. As a rule of thumb, set your iron on the cotton setting, but always test the temperature when working with white-on-white fabrics because they tend to scorch easily.

Develop the habit of pressing each seam as it is sewn. Turn the piece over and "tack press" by lightly touching the iron to the seam allowance to get it started in the right direction. On the front side, spray lightly and press with gentle pressure from the center out. Check the back of the block to make sure all seams are pressed correctly before proceeding.

APPLIQUÉ

Some of the projects in this book include appliquéd motifs, and full-size pattern pieces are provided. *These patterns do not include seam allowances.*

A placement guide is included with each project for guidance in positioning the appliqués. In some cases, this placement guide will also illustrate the finished project.

Two methods of appliqué follow. *Note that all appliqué templates are printed in reverse of how the motif appears in the finished project to make them suitable for the fusible-web technique. Be sure to flip over the templates if you plan to appliqué by hand.*

Fusible-Web Appliqué

Fusible-web appliqué is a quick, efficient alternative to the hand-appliqué method and gives the finished project a wonderful folk-art look. Each shape is traced directly onto a paper-backed fusible bonding agent, which is applied with an iron to the back side of the appliqué fabric. The shape is cut, and the paper removed. Then the fabric shape is heat-bonded to the background block and finished with a decorative hand or machine stitch.

There are many fusible products on the market. Experiment to find the one that best suits your needs, and be sure to read and follow the manufacturer's instructions.

Remember: Because the fusible is bonded to the back side of the fabric, the appliqué patterns for the projects in this book have been printed in reverse. When the shape is flipped over to be

Tip

Interface the lightest appliqué fabrics with woven, iron-on interfacing to keep darker underlayers or background fabrics from showing through.

bonded to the background, the appliqué appears correctly on the finished project.

1. Trace the appropriate appliqué patterns directly onto the fusible material; cut out around the traced designs, leaving a ⅛"-wide margin.
2. Fuse the traced designs to the back side of the appropriate appliqué fabrics, cut on the drawn lines, and remove the paper backing.
3. When the appliqué involves layers, fuse the layers before adhering them to the background. Use a Teflon pressing sheet to protect the fabric, the iron, and the ironing surface.
4. Refer to the placement guide or finished project illustration for guidance in positioning and pinning the appliqués to the background.
5. Machine stitch the fused design to the background, using a very short (⅛"-wide) zigzag or blanket stitch.

Note: If tear away stabilizer is required for a project, cut the stabilizer 1" or 2" larger than the appliqué and place the stabilizer between the project and the feed dogs. Typing or other lightweight paper may be used as a substitute stabilizer.

Hand Appliqué

Hand appliqué involves applying (or stitching) a motif to a background block or unit. It is done with an invisible stitch, using matching thread and a small (size #11 or #12), fine appliqué needle.

1. Transfer the appropriate pattern pieces to your preferred template material. *Remember:* Since the patterns are reversed for the fusible method, you'll need to turn them over for hand appliqué if they are asymmetrical.

2. Place the template on the right side of the fabric, reversing if necessary, and trace with a sharp pencil. Cut out the shape, adding a ¼"-wide seam allowance. After cutting, clip into the seam allowance on inside curves only.
3. Turn the fabric raw edge on the drawn line to the wrong side, and baste with a light-colored thread.

Tip

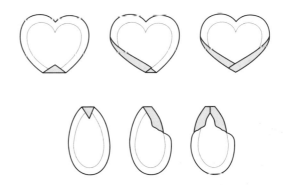

When basting points, such as the tip of a leaf or the bottom of a heart, fold the point back first, then fold over each side.

4. Pin the basted motifs in place, using the placement guide to position the pieces.
5. Appliqué the pieces. If the design involves layers, begin with the pieces on the bottom layer. Use thread that matches the color of the appliqué.

• Knot the thread and bring the needle up from the wrong side, through the background fabric, barely catching the folded edge of the appliqué.

2. Pull the thread through just until snug. The stitches lie close to the edges of the appliqué but should not be so tight that they pull or pucker the piece. Repeat, inserting the needle at evenly spaced intervals for a uniform edge as shown.

Blanket stitch

Stem Stitch

This stitch is great for making tiny stems, outlining, or adding detail. Knot the thread and bring the needle from the back to the front at A. Reinsert the needle at B and bring it out again at C as shown. Keep the embroidery floss above the needle as you take each stitch.

Satin Stitch

Fill in large areas quickly with this easy stitch. Knot the thread and bring the needle from the back to the front at A. Reinsert the needle at the opposite side of the shape you wish to fill at B as shown. Repeat until the desired area is completely covered with long stitches.

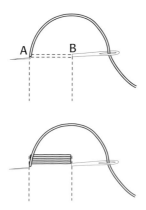

FINISHING

The following instructions will help you assemble finished blocks to make a quilt or wall hanging. Some of the techniques described—for example, easy-turn finishing—will also be used to complete various nursery accessories.

Adding Borders

Finished measurements of quilts and wall hangings may vary slightly due to personal cutting and sewing techniques. While specific border measurements are listed for the projects, I recommend that you double-check and adjust border measurements as necessary before sewing borders to your quilt. Carefully matching measurements helps to keep quilts square and avoid rippled borders.

Note: The borders for all projects in this book are straight rather than mitered.

1. Measure the quilt top through its vertical center. Cut side strips to that length. Mark the midpoints of both the side border strips and the quilt top. Place the border strips and quilt top right sides together, pinning to match ends and midpoints. Add additional pins to ease as necessary. Stitch the border strips to the quilt top with a ¼"-wide seam allowance and press the seams toward the border.

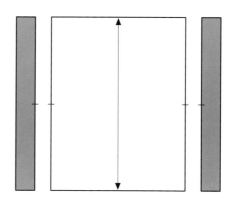

- Insert the needle into the background fabric beside the folded edge, as close as possible to the place where the thread came through the background fabric. Travel under the background fabric to make a tiny ⅛" stitch, then bring the needle once again through the background fabric and the appliqué's folded edge. Continue around the perimeter of the shape, making snug, even stitches. Use the point of the needle to turn and smooth the fabric on curved edges.

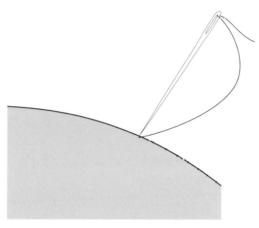

Bring the needle straight back down.

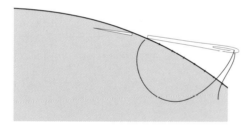

6. Finish with a knot on the back side of the block; remove the basting stitches.

EMBROIDERY STITCHES

Hand embroidery lends a touch of interest and texture to the finished project. It can also serve a practical purpose by securing an appliqué shape to the background fabric.

Blanket Stitch

This embroidery stitch has recently become popular again as an alternative to machine stitching to finish fusible appliqué. A row of blanket stitches around the edges of fused appliqué pieces gives them a finished look and prevents the edges from peeling up.

If you are planning to hand stitch your fusible appliqué, choose a light- or medium-weight fusible web that a needle can penetrate. Follow the manufacturer's instructions for fusing the appliqué pieces in place. Use a needle larger than you would normally use for hand embroidery and three strands of embroidery floss.

1. Knot the thread and bring it from the back to the front of the piece, coming out right next to the edge of the appliqué piece at A as shown. Insert the needle through all layers at B and bring the needle out at the edge of the appliqué piece at C. Loop the thread under the tip of the needle.

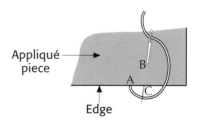

Appliqué piece

Edge

2. Measure the quilt top through its horizontal center, including the side borders. Cut the top and bottom border strips to that length. Mark the midpoints of both the border strips and the quilt top. Place the border strips and quilt top right sides together, pinning to match ends and midpoints. Add additional pins to ease as necessary. Stitch the border strips to the quilt top with a ¼"-wide seam allowance; press the seams toward the border.

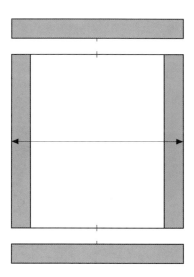

Choosing Batting and Backing

Choosing the right batting and backing for a project is just as important as the selection of fabric for the top. Consider durability, appearance, and the way the quilt will be used, cared for, and cleaned when making your decision.

Personal batting preferences vary. Take time to try different quilting techniques on different types and weights of batting to develop a feel for the look you want and the way the batting handles.

The batting choices for a wall hanging will be different than those made for a bed quilt. For wall hangings, choose a thin batting (100% cotton or cotton blend) that will hang flat against the wall. These ultra-thin battings can be machine or hand quilted.

For larger projects, high-loft polyester batting gives a fat, cushiony look. These thick battings are more difficult to needle, but can be machine quilted or tied. Low-loft cotton or cotton-blend batting gives a supple, traditional look, and is perfect for hand quilting.

While muslin is the traditional choice for backing, consider using a single print, or even piecing strips and scraps together until you have a backing of the desired size. Using a variety of fabrics is a great way to use leftovers and to create an interesting quilt back. Consider also whether you plan to machine or hand quilt your work. If you intend to hand quilt, choose a solid or almost-solid backing fabric to showcase your beautiful hand stitches, as well as one that allows a quilting needle to glide through comfortably. Do not use bed sheets for your backing since most sheets are difficult to push a needle through.

Cut the backing 4" larger than the size of the finished top. For large quilts, there are 90"and 108"-wide fabrics available. If it is necessary to piece the backing to get the necessary size, join two or three lengths of fabric as shown and press the seams open.

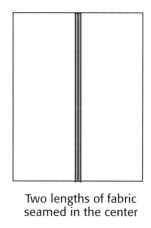

Two lengths of fabric seamed in the center

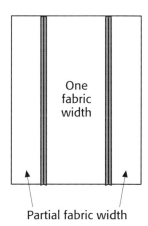

One fabric width

Partial fabric width

Assembling the Layers

"Sandwiching" is the term commonly used to describe joining the three quilt layers. Begin by laying the backing, wrong side up, on a flat surface, such as a tabletop or floor, and secure it with masking tape around all four edges. Take care to smooth out all the wrinkles, but don't distort it by pulling too tightly.

Next, smooth the batting on top of the backing. Make sure it covers the entire backing. Complete the "sandwich" by laying the quilt top, right side up, on the batting and smoothing out any wrinkles from the center to the outside edges.

Tip

If the batting is very wrinkled, spray it lightly with water and throw it into the dryer for approximately five minutes.

For smaller projects (or those you plan to quilt by machine), pin-baste with 1"-long rustproof safety pins. Space the pins approximately 4" apart, working from the center out and avoiding any marked quilting lines.

For larger projects (or those you plan to hand quilt), hand baste the layers together. Use a long needle and light-colored thread to take large stitches from the center to the quilt's outer top edge. Return to the center, basting in turn to the quilt's outer bottom edge, then to the right and left edges. Continue basting from the center out, creating a star-burst pattern.

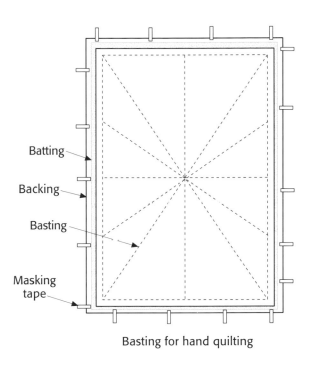

Basting for hand quilting

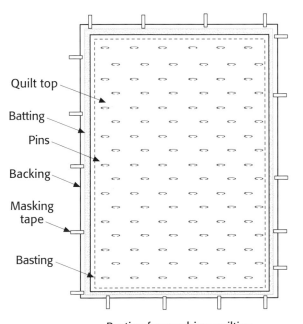

Basting for machine quilting

Quilting

For many of the projects in this book, you will be advised to machine or hand quilt your project "as desired." In the past, most quilts were quilted by hand. Today, quiltmakers have the advantage of choosing either method or a combination of both. Time and the intended use of the quilt are the usual deciding factors.

There are many excellent books to guide you, whether you choose to hand or machine quilt. *Loving Stitches* by Jeana Kimball offers expert instruction on hand quilting. For machine quilting, refer to *Machine Quilting Made Easy* by Maurine Noble. Both are published by That Patchwork Place/Martingale & Co. and are available through your local quilt shop or favorite mail-order source.

When the quilting is complete, remove the pins or long basting stitches and trim the batting and backing to the size of the quilt top.

Finishing the Edges

French Binding

One option for finishing the edges of your quilt or wall hanging is French binding. This binding, constructed from a double thickness of fabric, is attractive, sturdy, and wears well.

Use a ruler and rotary cutter to cut binding strips 2½" × 42". Be sure to cut perfectly straight across the width of the folded fabric. For each project, cut the required number of binding strips, and join them with a 45° diagonal seam as described here, using Mimi Dietrich's technique to distribute seam bulk smoothly over the quilt's edges.

1. Place 2 strips right sides together, crossing the ends at right angles as shown. Lay them on a flat surface and pin.

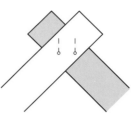

2. Imagine the strips as a large letter *A*, and draw a line across the strips to form the crossbar as shown. Sew directly on the line.

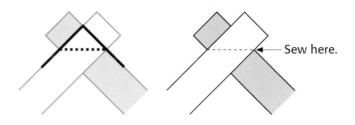

Sew here.

3. Trim the excess fabric, leaving a ¼"-wide seam allowance.

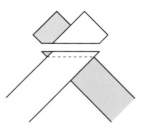

4. Press the seam open.

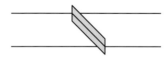

5. Fold the binding strips in half lengthwise, wrong sides together, and press.

6. To determine the length of the top and bottom bindings, measure the width of the quilt through its horizontal center and cut 2 strips to that measurement. Match the top and bottom raw edges of the quilt with the raw edges of the binding, right sides together. Pin, then sew the binding to the quilt with a ¼"-wide seam allowance. Fold the binding over the seam allowance to the back of the quilt and hand stitch in place along the seam line.

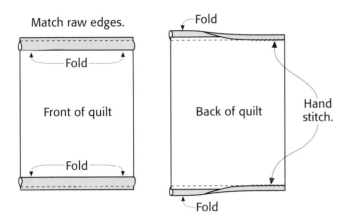

7. For the side bindings, measure the length of the quilt through its vertical center, add 1" to this measurement, and cut 2 binding strips to that length. For a clean finished edge, fold each end under ½" and press.

Sew the binding strips to the left and right sides of the quilt, and finish them in the same way as the top and bottom bindings were finished.

Easy-Turn Finishing

This simple "pillowcase" method will be used to finish the bumper pad and headboard in the various collections in *The Quilted Nursery*. It also makes a quick, no-fuss finish for quilts and wall hangings.

1. Trim the backing and batting to the same size as the project top. Place the project top and backing right sides together, with the backing as the top layer. Lay on the batting, carefully smoothing all layers and pin.
2. Unless otherwise noted, sew around the outside raw edges with a ¼"-wide seam allowance. Leave an opening large enough for

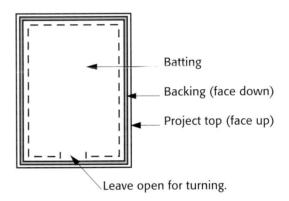

turning the project right side out.
3. Trim the excess seam allowance as necessary, clip the corners on the diagonal, and turn the project through the opening.
4. Press the project and slipstitch the opening closed.

Special Touches

Ruffles and piping add decorative flair to many of the projects in this book, while ties and tabs hold valances, bumper pads, and headboards securely in place. General construction techniques for these special touches are described here. Specific cutting and sewing requirements appear with the individual project instructions.

RUFFLES

1. Pin the ruffle strips, right sides together, end to end. Join the strips with a ¼"-wide seam allowance and press the seams open. Fold the short raw edges of each end over 1" to the wrong side and press.

    For pillow ruffles, sew ruffle strips together, end to end, to form a single long strip as described above. Place the raw edges of each end right sides together and sew with a ½"-wide seam allowance to form a circle. Press the seams open.

2. Fold the strip in half lengthwise, wrong sides together, aligning the raw edges; press.

3. Sew a long, machine gathering stitch ⅛" from the long raw edges through both layers as shown.

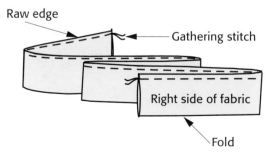

Raw edge
Gathering stitch
Right side of fabric
Fold

4. Measure and pin-mark ½" from each corner of the mattress base (for dust ruffles) or crib quilt, and ¾" from each end for headboards and bumper pads. Measure and divide the project into equal sections; mark with pins. Repeat to measure and pin-mark the ruffle. This gives you matching guidelines for joining the ruffle to the project.

5. Place the project top and the ruffle right sides together, aligning the raw edges. Gather and pin the ruffle to the project, adjusting the gathers evenly between the pinned sections.

6. Baste the ruffle in place with a ⅛"-wide seam allowance as shown.

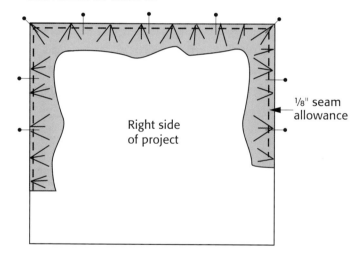

Right side of project

⅛" seam allowance

TIES

1. Fold each tie strip in half, wrong sides together, matching the long raw edges; press.

2. Open the strip, then refold the raw edges to meet at the center crease and press.

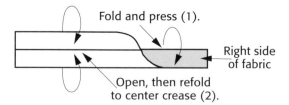

Fold and press (1).
Right side of fabric
Open, then refold to center crease (2).

3. Refold the strip along the center crease and topstitch close to the "double" folded edges.
4. Knot the ends or trim with pinking shears to finish.

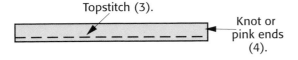

Topstitch (3).

Knot or pink ends (4).

TABS

These are stitched to the top edge of a valance to allow a rod to be inserted for hanging.

1. Fold each 3" × 6" tab strip in half right sides together, aligning the long raw edges.
2. Sew 1 short end and the long side with a 1/4"-wide seam allowance as shown.

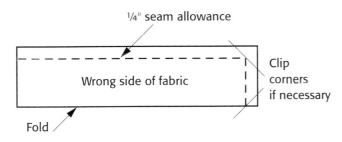

1/4" seam allowance

Wrong side of fabric

Clip corners if necessary

Fold

3. Trim the excess seam allowance as needed. Trim the stitched corners on the diagonal, turn the tab right side out, and press.
4. Space tabs evenly across the right side of the top edge of the project as shown. Begin 1/2" from each end of the project and align the raw edges of the project with the unfinished edge of the tab. Baste the tabs in place with a 1/8"-wide seam allowance.

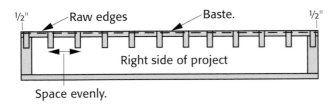

1/2"   Raw edges   Baste.   1/2"

Right side of project

Space evenly.

PIPING

1. Sew fabric strips end to end, right sides together, until you have achieved the required length for piping.
2. Center the piping on the wrong side of the long fabric strip. Fold the fabric over the piping, aligning the raw edges, and use a zipper foot to machine baste next to the piping.

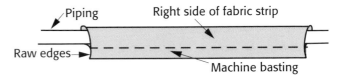

Piping   Right side of fabric strip

Raw edges

Machine basting

3. Cut the stitched piping into segments as directed by the specific project instructions.
4. Pull the piping out 3/4" from each end of the fabric tube and trim as shown. Stuff the cut end of the piping back in the tube, leaving 3/4" of fabric on each end free of piping.

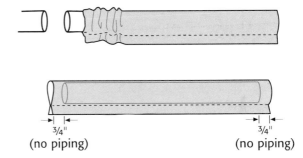

3/4"   3/4"
(no piping)   (no piping)

5. With right sides together and long raw edges aligned, pin the piping to the project and baste in place with a 1/8"-wide seam allowance.

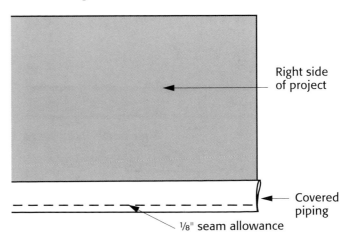

Right side of project

Covered piping

1/8" seam allowance

General Accessory Construction

The nursery accessories in *The Quilted Nursery* are simple and fun to construct for all skill levels. The basic construction for each accessory is listed below. The individual cutting and sewing requirements will be found in the specific project instructions.

BUMPER PAD

Use high-loft, bonded batting for all bumper pads.

1. Position the bumper pad in the crib. Mark the top and bottom tie-placement locations with pins, beginning ¾" from each end.
2. Fold the completed ties in half and press on the fold (see "Ties" on page 18). Align the folds with the raw edges of the right side of the bumper pad, on top of any ruffles or piping. Baste in place with a ⅛"-wide seam allowance.
3. Place the bumper backing pieces right sides together and sew end to end. Press the seams open and trim to the length of the front panel.
4. Use the easy-turn method and a ½"-wide seam allowance to finish the bumper pad (see "Easy-Turn Finishing" on page 17). Be sure

the ruffles and loose ends of the ties do not get caught in the seam.

HEADBOARD

Use high-loft, bonded batting for all headboards.

1. Transfer the pattern below to a 1" grid to make a template for the headboard.

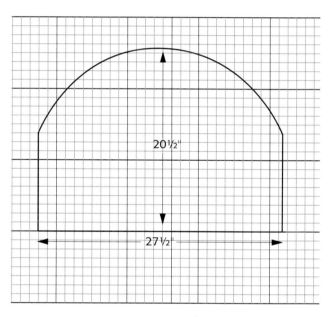

20½"

27½"

1 square = 1"
(pattern includes seam allowance)

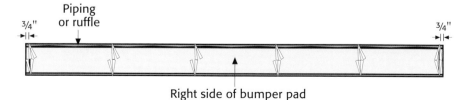

Piping or ruffle

¾"

¾"

Right side of bumper pad

2. Center the headboard template on the right side of the pieced headboard unit. Carefully trace around the template. Remove the template and machine baste ⅛" inside the traced line. Cut out on the traced line.

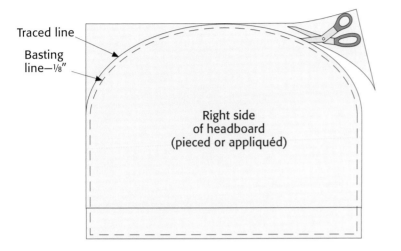

3. Make ruffles according to the project instructions, referring to "Ruffles" on page 18 for guidance.
4. With right sides together, align the raw edges of the ruffle and the curved edge of the headboard. Gather and pin the ruffle to the curved edge of the headboard, adjusting the gathers evenly between the pin marks. Baste the ruffle in place with a ⅛"-wide seam allowance.
5. Make ties according to the project instructions, referring to "Ties" on page 18 for guidance.

6. Position the headboard in the crib and pin-mark the tie-placement locations as suggested in the illustration. Bottom ties should be positioned ¾" from the bottom edge of the headboard.

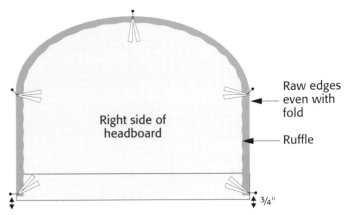

7. Fold the completed ties and press on the fold. Align the folded edge of the ties with the raw, curved edge of the headboard, right sides together and on top of any ruffles or piping.
8. Use the headboard template to cut 1 batting and 1 backing piece.
9. Use the easy-turn method and a ½"-wide seam allowance to finish the headboard (see "Easy-Turn Finishing" on page 17). Be sure the loose ends of the ties do not get caught in the seam.
10. Topstitch ¼" from the outside edge all around the headboard.

DUST RUFFLE

The dust ruffle in each of the collections in *The Quilted Nursery* finishes with a 16" drop, except for Sugar Bunny, which has a 19" drop.

The instructions given for each collection make a dust ruffle that fits a standard 27" × 52" crib mattress. Before you begin, measure the child's crib to determine any variations in the basic mattress base and ruffle drop so that you can adjust the specific project instructions to match your target measurements.

1. For the side ruffles, place 2 strips right sides together, end to end, and sew. Make 2 of these side ruffles. The head and foot ruffles use 1 strip each.
2. If the instructions call for a bottom border, repeat step 1, using the appropriate bottom border strips. Fold each of the assembled bottom border strips in half, wrong sides together, aligning the long raw edges; press.
3. With right sides together, align the long raw edges of the appropriate ruffle strip with the matching bottom border strip. Trim the short ends of the ruffle and border to the same length; pin and sew. Press the seam allowance toward the bottom border and topstitch the seam.
4. Hem the short ends of the bordered ruffles with a double ½" fold and topstitch.
5. Sew a double row of long, machine gathering stitches ¼" and ⅜" from the raw edge of the ruffle top.

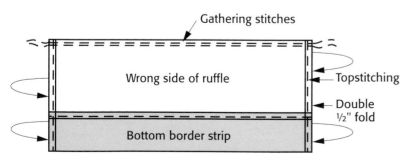

6. Taper the corners of the mattress base with a double ½" diagonal fold and topstitch as shown.

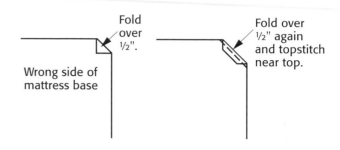

7. Gather the ruffle pieces to fit the mattress base. Space the gathers evenly and pin each ruffle right sides together with the appropriate side of the base. Machine stitch in place with a ½"-wide seam allowance.

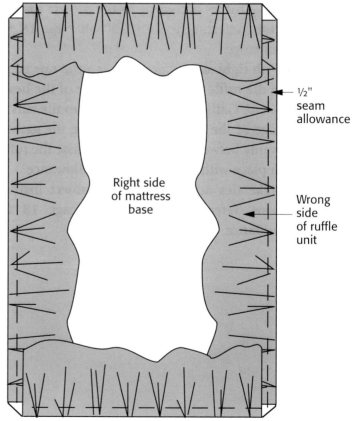

8. Fold the seam allowance toward the mattress base and topstitch on the right side to hold the seam allowance in place.

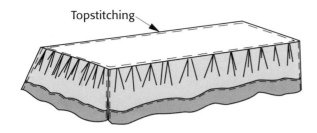
Topstitching

VALANCE LINING AND FINISHING

1. Place lining strips right sides together and sew end to end. Measure the horizontal width through the center of the valance and, unless directed otherwise, cut the lining strip to this measurement.
2. Place the pieced valance and the lining right sides together and sew with a ¼"-wide seam allowance as shown below. Leave a 6" opening on one side for turning.
3. Trim the seam allowance as necessary, clip the corners on the diagonal, and turn the valance right side out.
4. Press the valance and slipstitch the opening closed.
5. Topstitch the valance according to the specific project instructions.

PILLOW FINISHING

1. Layer the pillow top, right side up, on top of the batting; quilt as desired (see "Quilting" on page 16).
2. If the pillow includes a ruffle, refer to "Ruffles" on page 18 for guidance. Divide the entire perimeter of the pillow into even sections and mark with pins. Repeat for the ruffle.
3. Lay the pillow top and backing right sides together; sew ¼" all around the perimeter, leaving an opening for turning as shown below. Trim any excess seam allowance and clip the corners on the diagonal. Turn the pillow right side out, press, stuff it with filler or a pillow form, and slipstitch the opening closed.

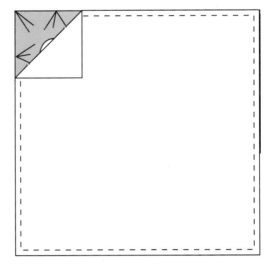

6" opening

Baby's Secret Garden

This whimsical collection, inspired by a century-old quilt, becomes "new again" thanks to today's trend of blending prints, solids, and stripes. The flower-garden theme runs throughout with Log Cabin block backgrounds and appliquéd flowers. This complete nursery features a crib quilt with a scalloped inner border, a headboard, bumper pad, dust ruffle, window valance, wall hanging, pillows, and even a diaper stacker. The secret? Only the little one knows, as he giggles and coos at this beautiful, blossoming "secret garden."

THE BASIC LOG CABIN BLOCK

Many of the projects in the Secret Garden collection include traditional-style Log Cabin blocks. The following instructions tell you how to construct the basic Log Cabin block. The directions for each project specify how many Log Cabin blocks to make.

You need small amounts of ten fabrics to make each block: five medium prints and/or solids and five light prints and/or solids. The specific project tells you exactly how much fabric you will need. The sample collection is made up in pastels, but you can choose any colors you wish.

It is essential to maintain an exact, consistent ¼"-wide seam allowance when constructing the Log Cabin block. Although the sewing is simple, there are many seams. This makes it easy for the block to finish too small or too large if you are not careful!

To help ensure accuracy, each Log Cabin strip for the block is cut exactly to size. Press the seam away from the center of the block as each strip is added, then measure the block. Adjust the seam allowances as needed.

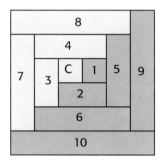

Finished Block Size: 9"

Cutting for One Block

From *each* medium and light fabric, cut:
   1 strip, 2" × 10"
From the 5 medium strips, randomly crosscut and label the following:
   1 square, 2" × 2" (#1)
   1 strip, 2" × 3½" (#2)
   1 strip, 2" × 5" (#5)
   1 strip, 2" × 6½" (#6)
   1 strip, 2" × 8" (#9)
   1 strip, 2" × 9½" (#10)
From the 5 light strips, randomly crosscut and label the following:
   1 square, 2" × 2" (C/center)
   1 strip, 2" × 3½" (#3)
   1 strip, 2" × 5" (#4)
   1 strip, 2" × 6½" (#7)
   1 strip, 2" × 8" (#8)

Assembling the Blocks

1. Lay out the entire block as shown in the block layout diagram.

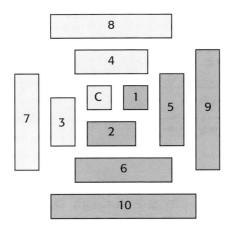

2. Sew #1 to C (the light center square); press the seam away from the center.

3. Add #2 to the bottom edge of the C/#1 unit and press. Continue adding strips clockwise in numeric sequence around the center square.

 BABY'S SECRET GARDEN BUMPER PAD

Finished Bumper Pad Size: 137½" × 11½"
Finished Block Size: 9"

Materials: (42"-wide fabric)

¼ yd. *each* of 5 different medium prints and/or solids for Log Cabin blocks

¼ yd. *each* of 5 different light prints and/or solids for Log Cabin blocks

½ yd. coordinating light/medium subtle print for Flower block backgrounds

¼ yd. medium green print for Flower block grass

⅛ yd. *each* of 3 different prints for appliqués*

⅞ yd. coordinating plaid, <u>check</u>, or stripe for borders and ties

⅞ yd. contrasting print for ruffle

1½ yds. fabric for backing

12" × 138" rectangle of high-loft bonded batting**

½ yd. lightweight fusible web

*Or use scraps to total ⅜ yd.
**Batting may be pieced.

Cutting

From *each* of the 5 medium and 5 light fabrics, cut:

    2 strips, each 2" × 42", for Log Cabin blocks

From the light/medium print, cut:

    2 strips, each 7" × 42", for Flower block background

From the medium green print, cut:

    2 strips, each 3" × 42", for Flower block grass

From the coordinating plaid, check, or stripe, cut:

    8 strips, each 1¾" × 42", for borders

    12 strips, each 2¼" × 20", for ties

From the contrasting print, cut:

    8 strips, each 3½" × 42", for ruffle

From the backing fabric, cut:

    4 strips, each 12" × 42"

Assembling the Log Cabin and Appliqué Blocks

You will need 8 basic Log Cabin blocks and 7 Flower appliqué blocks for the Baby's Secret Garden Bumper Pad.

1. Referring to "The Basic Log Cabin Block" on page 26, use the 2" × 42" light and medium strips to construct a total of 8 Log Cabin blocks.

2. Place a 7" × 42" background strip and a 3" × 42" grass strip right sides together, aligning one long raw edge. Pin and sew the strips together to make a background strip-pieced

unit. Press toward the grass strip. Make 2 of these units.

3. Crosscut the pieced strip unit into 9½"-wide segments as shown. Cut 7.

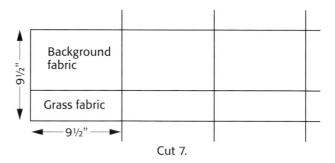

Cut 7.

4. Use the pattern pieces on page 133 to trace appliqué pieces A through D. Refer to the instructions for "Fusible-Web Appliqué" on page 10 to prepare, cut, fuse, and stitch the appliqués in place on the pieced background blocks. If you prefer, you may hand appliqué the flower motifs (see "Hand Appliqué" on page 11). You'll need to cut 14 A and 7 each of B, C, and D. Refer to the diagrams for guidance in positioning the pieces.

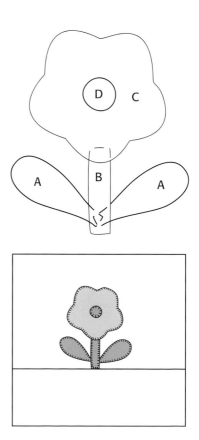

Assembling the Bumper Pad Panel

1. Arrange, then sew the blocks together as shown in the diagrams below, alternating a Log Cabin block with a Flower block as shown. Be sure that you are positioning the Log Cabin blocks correctly. Press the seams away from the Log Cabin blocks.

2. Place the 1¾"-wide border strips right sides together and sew them end to end to make one long continuous strip. Crosscut this strip into 2 strips, each 138" long, for the top and bottom borders, and 2 strips, each 9½" long, for the side borders.

3. Place the side border strips right sides together with the short sides of the panel; pin and sew. Press toward the border. Repeat to add the top and bottom border strips to the panel (see "Adding Borders" on page 13).

Finishing the Bumper Pad

1. Use the 2¼"-wide strips to construct 12 ties (see "Ties" on page 18).

2. Use the 3½" × 42" strips to construct a single long ruffle (see "Ruffles" on page 18).

3. Refer to the general instructions to add the ruffle and ties and to finish the bumper pad (see "Bumper Pad" on page 20). Notice in the second diagram below that the ruffle runs along only the top edge of the bumper pad, while the ties are along the top and bottom edges.

4. Quilt as desired. You might quilt beside the seam allowances (in-the-ditch) between the blocks and around the Log Cabin strips, outline the appliqués, and/or add any motifs you wish (see "Quilting" on page 16).

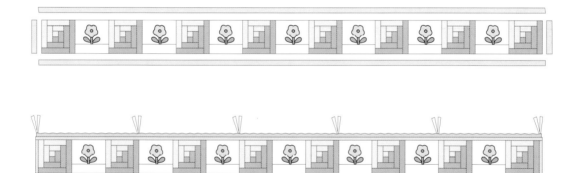

 ## BABY'S SECRET GARDEN WALL HANGING

Finished Quilt Size: 27" × 27"
Finished Block Size: 9"

Materials: (42"-wide fabric)

⅛ yd. *each* of 5 different medium prints and/or solids for Log Cabin blocks

⅛ yd. *each* of 5 different light prints and/or solids for Log Cabin blocks

⅛ yd. *total* of 3 different prints for appliqués*

⅜ yd. bright, contrasting print or solid for accent border

½ yd. coordinating print for outer border

1 yd. fabric for backing

⅓ yd. fabric for binding

30" × 30" square of batting

⅛ yd. lightweight fusible web

*Or use scraps.

Cutting

From *each* of the 5 medium and 5 light fabrics, cut:

    1 strip, 2" × 42", for Log Cabin blocks

From the bright, contrasting print or solid, cut:

    2 strips, each 2" × 18½", for side accent borders

    2 strips, each 2" × 21½", for top and bottom accent borders

From the coordinating print, cut:

    2 strips, each 3½" × 21½", for side outer borders

    2 strips, each 3½" × 27½", for top and bottom outer borders

From the backing fabric, cut:

    1 square, 34" × 34"

From the binding fabric, cut:

    4 strips, each 2½" × 42"

Assembling the Quilt Top

You will need 4 basic Log Cabin blocks for the Baby's Secret Garden Wall Hanging. These blocks are sewn together and used as background for the flower appliqués.

1. Referring to "The Basic Log Cabin Block" on page 26, use the 2" × 42" light and medium strips to construct a total of 4 Log Cabin blocks.

2. Arrange the blocks as shown in the diagram at right. Be certain that the blocks are positioned as shown, with the darker side of the blocks toward the outer edges of the quilt top. Refer to the project photo on page 30 for additional guidance.

3. Sew the blocks together in 2 horizontal rows of 2 blocks each. Press the center seam allowances in opposing directions; pin, then sew the 2 rows together to form the center of the wall hanging top (see "Matching Points" on page 8).

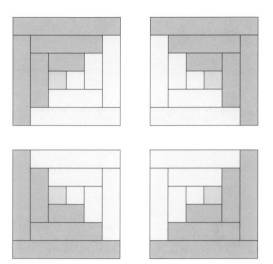

4. Use the pattern pieces on page 133 to trace appliqué pieces A through D. Refer to the instructions for "Fusible-Web Appliqué" on page 10 to prepare, cut, fuse, and stitch the appliqués in place in the center of the pieced Log Cabin blocks as shown in the diagram on page 32. If you prefer, you may hand appliqué the flower motifs (see "Hand Appliqué" on page 11). You'll need to cut 4 A and 2 each of B, C, and D to complete the 2 flower appliqués. Refer to the diagrams on page 28 and the wall hanging photo on page 30 for additional guidance in placing the appliqués.

5. Place the side accent border strips right sides together with the left and right raw edges of the quilt; pin, then sew the border strips to the quilt. Press the seam allowances toward the border. Repeat to add the top and bottom accent border strips, then the side, top, and bottom outer borders to the quilt top (see "Adding Borders" on page 13).

Finishing the Quilt

1. Layer the backing, batting, and quilt top for basting and baste the 3 layers (see "Assembling the Layers" on page 15).
2. Quilt as desired (see "Quilting" on page 16).
3. Use the 2½" × 42" strips to make binding. Bind to finish (see "French Binding" on page 16).

BABY'S SECRET GARDEN HEADBOARD

Finished Headboard Size: 27" × 20"
Finished Block Size: 9"

Materials: (42"-wide fabric)

¼ yd. *each* of 5 different medium prints and/or solids for Log Cabin blocks
¼ yd. *each* of 5 different light prints and/or solids for Log Cabin blocks
⅛ yd. *total* of 3 different prints for appliqués*
⅛ yd. coordinating medium print for bottom border
¼ yd. coordinating print for ties
½ yd. bright contrasting print for ruffle
⅞ yd. fabric for backing
30" × 30" square of high-loft, bonded batting
¼ yd. lightweight fusible web

*Or use scraps.

Cutting

From *each* of the 5 medium and 5 light fabrics, cut:
    2 strips, each 2" × 42", for Log Cabin blocks
From the medium coordinating print, cut:
    1 strip, 3" × 27½", for bottom border
From the coordinating print, cut:
    5 strips, each 2¼" × 20", for ties
From the bright contrasting print, cut:
    4 strips, each 3½" × 42", for ruffle
From the backing fabric, cut:
    1 square, 30" × 30"

Assembling the Blocks

You will need 6 basic Log Cabin blocks for the Baby's Secret Garden Headboard. Three of these blocks are embellished with flower appliqués.

1. Referring to "The Basic Log Cabin Block" on page 26, use the 2" × 42" medium and light strips to construct a total of 6 Log Cabin blocks.

2. Use the pattern pieces on page 133 to trace appliqué pieces A, C, D, and E. Refer to the instructions for "Fusible-Web Appliqué" on page 10 to prepare, cut, fuse, and stitch the appliqués in place on 3 of the pieced Log Cabin blocks. If you prefer, you may hand appliqué the flower motifs (see "Hand Appliqué" on page 11). You'll need to cut 6 A and 3 each of C, D, and E. Refer to the diagrams on page 28 (substituting E for B) and the diagram at right for guidance in positioning the appliqués. Notice that the Log Cabin blocks are all turned so that the dark strips appear on the same side of the block.

Constructing the Headboard Panel

1. Arrange the blocks as shown in the diagram on page 33, placing the 3 appliquéd blocks in the bottom row. Be certain that all Log Cabin blocks are turned so that the dark strips appear on the same side of the block. Refer to the project photo on page 33 for additional guidance. Sew the blocks in 2 horizontal rows of 3 blocks each, pressing the seam allowances in opposing directions (see "Machine Piecing" on page 8). Join the rows, pinning carefully to match the seams.

2. With right sides together, align the long raw edge of the bottom border strip to the bottom raw edge of the pieced headboard panel. Pin, sew, and press the seam allowance toward the border strip.

Finishing the Headboard

1. Use the 2¼"-wide strips to construct 5 ties (see "Ties" on page 18).
2. Use the 3½" × 42" strips to construct a single long ruffle (see "Ruffles" on page 18).
3. Refer to the general instructions to add the ruffle and ties and to finish the headboard (see "Headboard" on page 20). Notice that the ruffle runs along only the top curved edge of the headboard. Position the ties as shown.
4. Quilt as desired (see "Quilting" on page 16). Refer to the diagram for quilting suggestions.

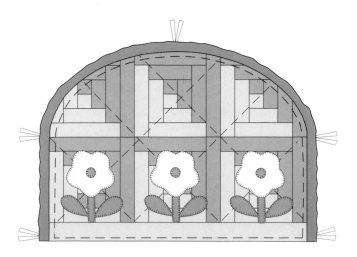

🌸 BABY'S SECRET GARDEN VALANCE

Finished Valance Size: 58" × 13"
Finished Block Size: 9"

Materials: (42"-wide fabric)

¼ yd. *each* of 5 different medium prints and/or solids for Log Cabin blocks
¼ yd. *each* of 5 different light prints and/or solids for Log Cabin blocks
⅛ yd. *total* of 3 different prints for appliqués*
½ yd. of coordinating medium print for borders
1½ yds. coordinating print or solid for lining
½ yd. *total* of 3 different prints for ties**
¼ yd. lightweight fusible web

*Or use scraps to total approximately ⅛ yard.
**Or use scraps to total approximately ½ yard.

Cutting

From *each* of the 5 medium and 5 light fabrics, cut:
    2 strips, each 2" × 42", for Log Cabin blocks
From the coordinating medium print, cut:
    2 strips, each 3" × 42", for top border
    2 strips, each 2" × 42", for bottom border
    2 strips, each 2½" × 9½", for side borders
From the coordinating print or solid, cut:
    2 strips, each 5" × 42", for lining header strip
    2 strips, each 18" × 42", for lining
From the 3 different prints, cut:
    9 strips *total*, each 2¼" × 20", for ties

Assembling the Valance Panel

You will need 6 basic Log Cabin blocks to complete the Baby's Secret Garden Valance. The lining header is embellished with 8 flower appliqués.

1. Referring to "The Basic Log Cabin Block" on page 26, use the 2" × 42" medium and light strips to construct a total of 6 Log Cabin blocks.

2. Arrange, then sew the blocks together in a single horizontal row as shown in the diagram. Be sure you are positioning the Log Cabin blocks correctly. Refer to the project photo above for additional guidance.

3. Place the 3" × 42" top border strips right sides together and sew them end to end to make one long continuous strip. Trim this long strip to measure 58½". Repeat for the 2" × 42" bottom border strips, the 5" × 42" lining header strips, and the 18" × 42" lining strips.

4. Place the side border strips right sides together with the short sides of the panel; pin and sew. Press toward the border. Repeat to add the top and bottom border strips to the panel (see "Adding Borders" on page 13). Finish the panel by placing the long raw edge of the lining header right sides together with the top raw edge of the bordered panel. Pin, sew, and press toward the panel.

Lining and Finishing the Valance

1. Use the 18" × 58½" lining strip to line the valance (see "Valance Lining and Finishing" on page 23).

2. Topstitch with a ¼"-wide seam all around the valance as shown.

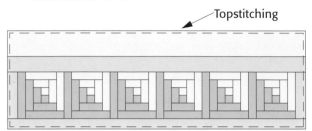

Topstitching

3. Use the pattern pieces on page 133 to trace appliqué pieces C and D. Refer to the instructions for "Fusible-Web Appliqué" on page 10 to prepare, cut, fuse, and stitch the appliqués in place on the back side of the valance as shown. If you prefer, you may hand appliqué the flower motifs (see "Hand Appliqué" on page 11). You'll need to cut 8 each of C and D. The flowers should be evenly spaced along the top edge of the lining, just inside the topstitching.

4. Use a yardstick and a disappearing or water-soluble marker to lightly mark a horizontal line on the back of the lining. This line should fall about 4½" from the top edge of the lining and correspond with the seam line where the lining header and the top border meet on the front side.

Marked "seam" line

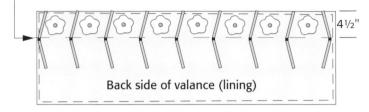

4½"

Back side of valance (lining)

5. Use the 2¼"-wide strips to construct 9 ties (see "Ties" on page 18).

6. Evenly space the 9 ties along the marked horizontal "seam" line. Pin the ties to secure them, then machine stitch each in place with an **X**. Knot the ends or trim them with pinking shears to finish.

7. Fold the lining header to the front side of the valance along the marked "seam" line and tie onto a decorative rod.

Flip lining header to front side of valance.

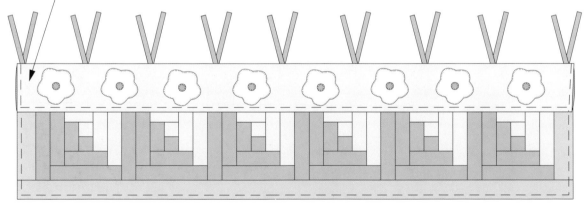

 ## BABY'S SECRET GARDEN DUST RUFFLE

Finished Mattress Base Size: 27" × 52"
Finished Drop Length: 16"

Materials: (42"-wide fabric)

1 5/8 yds. muslin or a flat crib sheet for mattress base

2 3/8 yds. light/medium plaid, check, stripe, or other print for ruffle

1 3/4 yds. coordinating medium print for bottom border

1/8 yd. *each* of 3 different prints for appliqués*

7/8 yd. of lightweight fusible web

*Or use scraps to total approximately 3/8 yd.

Cutting

Note: Adjust cutting instructions as needed to match crib measurements (see "Dust Ruffle" on page 22). Seam allowances are 1/4" wide.

From the muslin or flat crib sheet, cut:
    1 panel, 28" × 53", for mattress base
From the light/medium print, cut:
    6 strips, each 12 1/2" × 42", for ruffle
From the coordinating medium print, cut:
    6 strips, each 9" × 42", for bottom border

Constructing the Dust Ruffle

1. Refer to "Dust Ruffle," steps 1–4, on page 22 to construct the basic dust ruffle. Use the 12½"-wide strips for the ruffle, and the 9"-wide strips for the bottom border.

2. Use the pattern pieces on page 133 to trace appliqué pieces A, C, D, and E. Refer to the instructions for "Fusible-Web Appliqué" on page 10 to prepare, cut, fuse, and stitch the appliqués in place on the ruffle. If you prefer, you may hand appliqué the flower motifs (see "Hand Appliqué" on page 11). You'll need to cut 60 A and 30 each of C, D, and E. Refer to the diagrams on page 28, the project photo on page 37, and the diagram below for guidance in placing 10 flower appliqués on each side ruffle, and 5 on each of the top and bottom ruffles. The flowers sit along the seam line that joins the ruffle to the bottom border.

3. Refer to "Dust Ruffle," steps 5–8, on pages 22–23 to finish the dust ruffle.

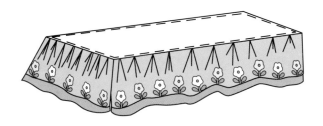

BABY'S SECRET GARDEN CRIB QUILT

Finished Quilt Size: 36½" × 45½"
Finished Block Size: 9"

Materials: (42"-wide fabric)

1 yd. light/medium plaid, check, or stripe for background
¾ yd. light contrasting print or solid for scalloped border
⅛ yd. *each* of 3 different prints for appliqués*
¼ yd. medium large-scale print for accent border
½ yd. coordinating light/medium print for outer border
1⅜ yds. fabric for backing
½ yd. fabric for binding
Crib-size batting (45" × 60")
½ yd. lightweight fusible web

*Or use scraps to total approximately ⅜ yd.

Cutting

From the light/medium plaid, check, or stripe, cut:
    1 panel, 28½" × 37½", for background
From the light contrasting print or solid, cut:
    4 strips, each 5" × 42", for scalloped border
From the medium large-scale print, cut:
    2 strips, each 1½" × 37½", for side accent border
    2 strips, each 1½" × 30½", for top and bottom accent border
From the coordinating light/medium print, cut:
    2 strips, each 3½" × 39½", for side outer border
    2 strips, each 3½" × 36½", for top and bottom outer border
From the backing fabric, cut:
    1 rectangle, 40" × 50"
From the binding fabric, cut:
    5 strips, each 2½" × 42"

This quilt features a garden of fabric flowers framed by a delicate scalloped border. Both the flowers and the scalloped border may be hand appliquéd or applied with the fusible-web appliqué method. Review the options before you begin (see "Appliqué" on page 10). Remember to add a ¼"-wide seam allowance to the fabric pieces you cut for the flower motifs if you plan to hand appliqué. You'll also need to add seam allowances to the curved and short angled edges of the scalloped border pieces. No additional seam allowance is required for the fusible-web method. Refer to the quilt photo on page 39 for fabric suggestions.

1. Use the pattern on page 134 to make a template for the scalloped border. Join the pattern sections at the dotted lines to complete the pattern.

2. Cut 2 long side borders and 2 shorter top and bottom borders from the 5" × 42" strips. Be sure to place the appropriate fold line on the fabric fold as you cut each strip.

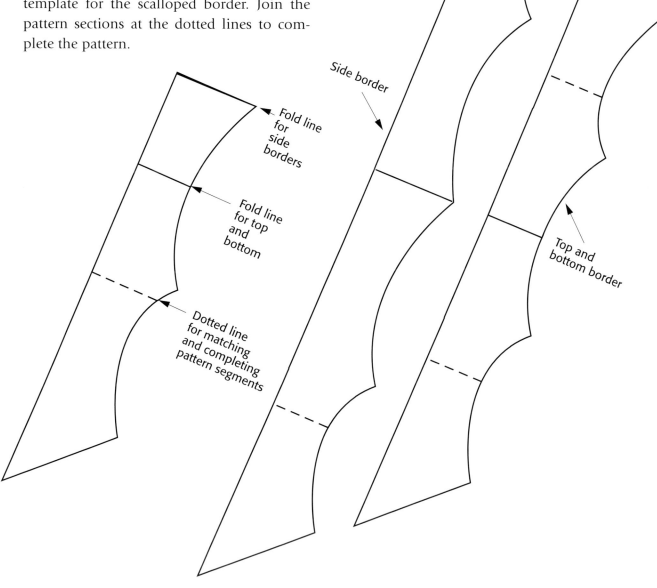

Fold line for side borders

Fold line for top and bottom

Dotted line for matching and completing pattern segments

Side border

Top and bottom border

3. To hand appliqué the scalloped border, lay out the 4 border scallops as they will appear in the quilt. Place 2 adjacent borders right sides together, aligning the short angled raw edges. Pin and stitch with a ¼"-wide seam allowance and press the seam open. Repeat until all 4 corner seams have been sewn.

4. Baste the seam allowance all around the long curved edge of the border piece (see "Hand Appliqué" on page 11). Lay the basted scalloped border, right side up, on the right side of the background panel, matching the outside raw edges. Baste around the outside edges to secure the border, then appliqué in place.

5. If you are fusing rather than appliquéing the borders, simply place the appropriate border, right side up, on the matching edge of the center panel. Align the long, straight raw edges, and butt the angled corners. Fuse in place and finish with decorative stitching (see "Fusible-Web Appliqué" on page 10).

6. Use the pattern pieces on page 133 to trace appliqué pieces A through D. Refer to the instructions for your preferred method of appliqué to prepare, cut, and apply the motifs to the center panel. You'll need to cut 20 A and 10 each of B, C, and D. Refer to the diagrams on page 28, the quilt photo on page 39, and the diagram at right for guidance in positioning the pieces. The base of each flower stem rests on the edge of the scalloped border.

7. Place the side accent border strips right sides together with the left and right raw edges of the quilt; pin, then sew the border strips to the quilt. Press the seam allowances toward the border. Repeat to add the top and bottom accent border strips, then the side, top, and bottom outer border strips to the quilt top (see "Adding Borders" on page 13).

Finishing the Quilt

1. Layer the backing, batting, and quilt top for basting and baste the 3 layers (see "Assembling the Layers" on page 15).
2. Quilt as desired (see "Quilting" on page 16).
3. Use the 2½" × 42" strips to make binding. Bind to finish (see "French Binding" on page 16).

BABY'S SECRET GARDEN DIAPER STACKER

Finished Project Size: 26½" × 13"

Materials: (42"-wide fabric)

The sample was sewn from 4 coordinating print fabrics. Try combining checks, stripes, florals, and other prints in your nursery colors.

¾ yd. print fabric #1 for stacker bag
⅜ yd. print fabric #2 for stacker top
½ yd. print fabric #3 for stacker bottom, bottom insert, and hanger
⅛ yd. print fabric #4 for piping cover and leaf and stem appliqués
⅞ yd. of ¾" piping
1 yd. ball fringe in a matching color
Small print scraps for flower appliqué
Small scraps of lightweight fusible web
½ yd. fusible interfacing
9" × 13" rectangle of corrugated cardboard
1 child's hanger
Batting scraps to cover hanger

Cutting

Use the pattern on page 135 to make a template for the stacker top (F). *The pattern includes a ⅝"-wide seam allowance.*

From print fabric #1, cut:
   2 rectangles, each 21" × 22¼", for stacker bag
From print fabric #2, cut:
   2 F for stacker top
From print fabric #3, cut:
   1 rectangle, 9⅝" × 13⅝", for stacker bottom
   1 rectangle, 13⅝" × 18⅝", for stacker bottom insert
From print fabric #4, cut:
   1 strip, 1¾" × 42", for piping cover
From the interfacing, cut:
   2 F for stacker top
   1 rectangle, 9⅝" × 13⅝", for stacker bottom

Constructing the Stacker Top

Note: Use a ⅝" wide seam allowance for all sewing steps.

1. To construct the top section of the stacker bag, fuse an interface F piece to the wrong side of each fabric F piece. These will be the front and back stacker top panels.

2. Use the pattern pieces on page 133 to trace appliqué pieces A through D. Refer to the instructions for "Fusible-Web Appliqué" on page 10 to prepare, cut, fuse, and stitch the appliqués in place on the front panel of the stacker top. If you prefer, you may hand appliqué the flower motifs (see "Hand Appliqué" on page 11). You'll need to cut 2 A and 1 each of B, C, and D. Refer to the diagrams on page 28, the project photo on page 43, and the diagram below for assistance in placing the appliqués.

3. Refer to the general instructions to construct the covered piping. Cut the covered piping to fit the outside curve of the top front panel (see "Piping" on page 19).

4. Matching the raw edges, pin the covered piping right sides together with the outside curve of the top front panel. Baste with a ⅛"-wide seam allowance.

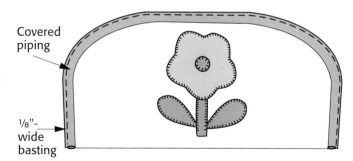

Covered piping

⅛"-wide basting

5. Place the front and back panels right sides together and pin. Sew around the outside edge of the curve with a ⅝"-wide seam allowance, leaving a ½" opening in the top center. *Do not sew the straight bottom edge.* Trim the seam allowance as necessary, turn the unit right side out, and press.

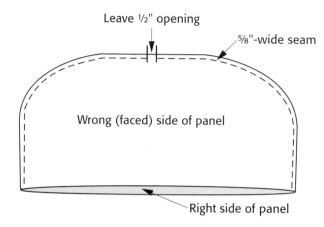

Leave ½" opening

⅝"-wide seam

Wrong (faced) side of panel

Right side of panel

Assembling the Stacker Bag

1. Place the 21" × 22¼" rectangles right sides together, aligning the raw edges. Pin and sew along one 21" edge; press the seam open. Turn the long, unseamed edges from the front to the wrong side of the panel to make a ¼" hem; press. Turn these finished edges a second time to form a 1" hem; press and finish with topstitching. Machine stitch ⅝" from the bottom edge of the bag for reinforcement.

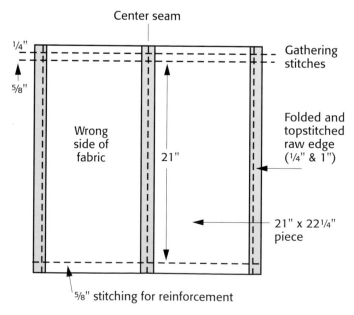

Center seam

¼"

⅝"

Gathering stitches

Wrong side of fabric

Folded and topstitched raw edge (¼" & 1")

21"

21" x 22¼" piece

⅝" stitching for reinforcement

2. Machine baste 2 rows of gathering stitches along the top edge. The first row should be approximately ¼" from the raw edge; the second should be just inside the ⅝" seam line.

3. To construct the stacker bottom, fuse the 9⅝" × 13⅝" piece of interfacing to the wrong side of the 9⅝" × 13⅝" fabric bottom piece. Place the fused bottom piece and the bottom raw edge of the bag right sides together. Match the center back seam of the stacker with the center back of the bottom piece. The bottom edge of the bag will not reach completely around the bottom piece. There will be a gap of approximately 4". Sew with a ⅝" seam, trim the seam allowances as necessary, and turn the bag right side out.

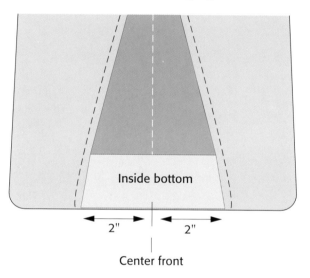

Inside bottom

2"   2"

Center front

4. Place the stacker top and the stacker bag right sides together, aligning the raw edges. Pin the bag to the top, matching the center seam of the bag with the center back of the top panel. The hemmed edges of the bag should meet at the center front of the top panel. Adjust the gathers evenly to fit. Baste; then stitch with a ⅝"-wide seam allowance.

5. Beginning at the back center seam, pin the ball fringe in place around the stacker, covering the seam where the top and the bag are joined. Tuck the starting and finishing ends under for a smooth connection and stitch the fringe in place.

6. To make the cover for the bottom insert, press $5/8$" under to the wrong side on one long edge of the $13^5/8$" × $18^5/8$" bottom insert piece. Fold the strip in half, right sides together, so the short raw edges meet. Pin, then stitch the 2 "unfinished" edges (exposed raw edges) with a $5/8$"-wide seam allowance. Turn the cover right side out and press. Insert the rectangle of cardboard and slipstitch the opening closed. Place the covered insert in the bottom of the stacker.

Covering the Hanger

1. To determine the width of the child's hanger hook, push the hook through a piece of paper and measure the diameter of the hole. Add $1/2$" for seam allowance.

2. Measure the length of the *hook* of the child's hanger and add 3". Cut 1 piece of print fabric #3 to this width by length measurement.

3. Turn both short ends of the strip under $1/2$" to the wrong side of the fabric and press. Fold the strip in half, right sides together, matching the long raw edges. Starting from one *short* folded edge, mark the fabric to indicate the *actual length* of the hook, and stitch to this point with a $1/4$"-wide seam allowance. Trim seam allowances as necessary and turn the hook cover right side out.

4. Measure the length of the *hanger*, and cut 1 piece of print fabric #3 to measure $6^1/4$" by double the length of the hanger.

5. Wrap the hanger (not the hook) with batting.

6. "Thread" the hook cover on the hanger hook. Tie the unstitched "tails" around the batting to secure the hook cover to the hanger.

7. To construct the hanger cover, press under a $5/8$" hem on both long edges of the cover strip. With right sides together, fold the strip, aligning the long "hemmed" edges. Stitch the short ends closed, trim the seam allowances as necessary, and turn the cover right side out.

8. Fold the hanger cover to find and pin-mark the midpoint on its long top and bottom edges. Beginning at one end of the top edge and then the other, sew a gathering stitch to the center pin. Wrap the gathering threads around the pin. Repeat for the bottom edge, again stopping at the center pin and wrapping the threads.

9. Insert the hanger into the hanger cover, matching the hook and the center point. Gather the cover to fit the hanger. Tie off and bury the gathering threads.

10. Insert the covered hanger in the diaper stacker.

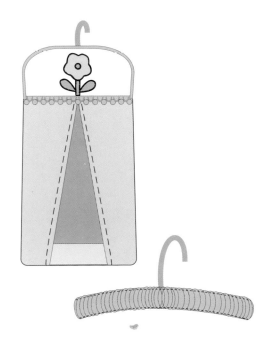

BABY'S SECRET GARDEN PILLOW

Finished Pillow Size: 12" square (plus ruffle)

Materials: (42"-wide fabric)

⅓ yd. light/medium subtle print for background
⅛ yd. medium green print for grass
⅛ yd. *each* of 3 different prints for appliqués*
⅓ yd. medium contrasting print for ruffle
½ yd. fabric for backing
12½" × 12½" square of batting
⅛ yd. lightweight fusible web**
Bag of polyester fiberfill or a 12" pillow form

*Or use scraps to total 3/8 yd.
**Or use scraps.

Cutting

From the light/medium print, cut:
    1 strip, 9½" × 12½", for background
From the medium green print, cut:
    1 strip, 3½" × 12½", for grass
From the medium contrasting print, cut:
    2 strips, each 4½" × 42, for ruffle
From the backing fabric, cut:
    1 square, 12½" × 12½"

Constructing the Pillow Top

1. Use the pattern pieces on page 133 to trace appliqué pieces A through E. Refer to the instructions for "Fusible-Web Appliqué" on page 10 to prepare, cut, fuse, and stitch the appliqués in place. If you prefer, you may hand appliqué the flower motifs (see "Hand Appliqué" on page 11). You'll need to cut 4 A, 1 each of B and E, and 2 each of C and D. Refer to the diagrams on page 28, the project photo on page 46, and the diagram below for guidance in placing the flower appliqués on the background.

2. With right sides together, align one long edge of the grass with the bottom edge of the appliquéd block; pin and sew. Press the seam allowance toward the grass.

Finishing the Pillow

1. Use the two 4½"-wide strips to construct a single long ruffle (see "Ruffles" on page 18).

2. Refer to "Pillow Finishing" on page 23 to complete the project.

Bright and Shining Pinwheels

Little girls and boys of all ages are fascinated with pinwheels. In this collection, the old favorite Pinwheel block takes on a new attitude with today's beautiful, bright, bold fabrics. There's a crib quilt with matching dust ruffle, pillows, bumper pad, headboard, wall hanging, and window valance. Just for fun, I've included a pinwheel decoration and a fabric-covered papier-mâché box. Try this collection to create a room decor that baby won't outgrow for many years to come!

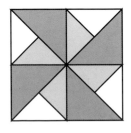 **THE BASIC PINWHEEL BLOCK**

Both the Bright and Shining Pinwheels collection, and the One Little Duck collection that follows it, feature the traditional Pinwheel block. The following instructions explain how to construct the basic block. The directions for each project tell you how many Pinwheel blocks to make.

You need just a small amount of three fabrics for each block: a light, a medium, and a dark. The light is used for the block background, and the dark for the large pinwheel triangles. These two fabrics remain consistent for all the blocks in each project. The medium is used for the small pinwheel triangles. (*Exception:* Mom's Utility Bag on page 86). When the project calls for multiple blocks, the medium fabric requirement will specify from three to five different medium fabrics.

Finished Block Size: 6"

Cutting for One Block

From the light fabric, cut:
    1 square, 4¼" × 4¼", for background
From the medium fabric, cut:
    1 square, 4¼" × 4¼", for small pinwheel
From the dark fabric, cut:
    2 squares, each 3⅞" × 3⅞", for large pinwheel

Assembling the Block

1. Place the light and medium squares right sides together. Draw a diagonal line across the medium square in both directions to make an X as shown.

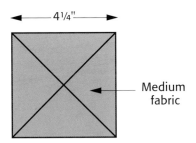

4¼"

Medium fabric

Always mark on medium square.

Note: Always mark on the medium fabric so that all the pinwheels turn in the same direction.

2. Sew ¼" from one side of the drawn lines exactly as shown.

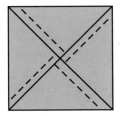

3. Cut the block apart on the drawn lines; press the seams toward the medium triangles.

4. Layer the 2 dark squares. Cut them from corner to corner on one diagonal to make a total of 4 dark triangles, 2 from each square.

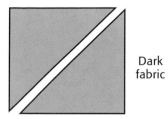

Dark fabric

5. Place a dark triangle right sides together with a light-medium triangle unit; pin and stitch. Press the seam allowance toward the dark triangle. Make 4.

Make 4.

6. Lay out the block as shown, making sure that you have positioned the pieced squares so that the pinwheel spins correctly. Piece the squares into 2 rows of 2 blocks each, pressing the seams toward the large dark triangle.

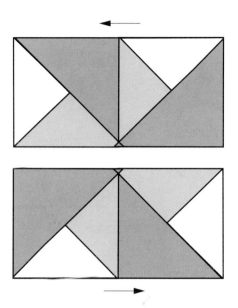

7. Place the 2 halves of the block right sides together, pinning carefully to match the center points (see "Machine Piecing" on page 80). Stitch, then press.

BRIGHT AND SHINING PINWHEELS BUMPER PAD

Finished Bumper Pad Size: 137½" × 11½"
Finished Block Size: 6"

Materials: (42"-wide fabric)

⅓ yd. light print or solid for background
¼ yd. *each* of 5 different medium prints and/or solids for small pinwheel triangles
½ yd. dark print or solid for large pinwheel triangles
⅞ yd. medium print for setting triangles
½ yd. contrasting print or solid for accent border
⅞ yd. bright print for ruffle
Assorted medium scraps to total ½ yd. for ties
1½ yds. fabric for backing
12" × 138" rectangle of high-loft, bonded batting*

*Batting may be pieced.

Cutting

From the light print or solid, cut:
15 squares, each 4¼" × 4¼", for background
From *each* of the 5 medium fabrics, cut:
3 squares, each 4¼" × 4¼", for small pinwheels
From the dark print or solid, cut:
30 squares, each 3⅞" × 3⅞", for large pinwheels
From the medium print, cut:
2 squares, each 5¼" × 5¼", for end setting triangles (A)
7 squares, each 9¾" × 9¾", for setting triangles (B)
2 rectangles, each 5½" × 9", for bumper pad ends
From the contrasting print or solid, cut:
8 strips, each 2" × 42", for accent border
From the bright print, cut:
8 strips, each 3½" × 42", for ruffle

From the assorted scraps, cut:
   12 strips *total*, each 2¼" × 20", for ties
From the backing fabric, cut:
   4 strips, each 12" × 42"

Assembling the Bumper Pad Panel

You will need 15 basic Pinwheel blocks for the Bright and Shining Pinwheels Bumper Pad.

1. Referring to "The Basic Pinwheel Block" on page 50, use the 4¼" light and medium squares and the 3⅞" dark squares to make a total of 15 Pinwheel blocks.
2. Cut each of the 5¼" squares on the diagonal in one direction to make a total of 4 end-setting triangles, 2 from each square. Label these A.
3. Cut each of the 9¾" squares on the diagonal in both directions to make a total of 28 setting triangles, 4 from each square. Label these B.
4. With right sides together, pin and sew the long diagonal side of an A triangle to 2 adjacent sides of a Pinwheel block as shown. Press toward the A triangles. With right sides together, pin and sew the short side of a B triangle to the Pinwheel block as shown. Press toward the B triangle. Make 2 and label these Unit 1.

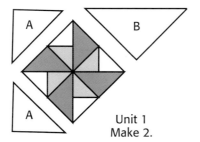

Unit 1
Make 2.

5. With right sides together, pin and sew the short side of a B triangle to opposite sides of a Pinwheel block as shown. Press toward the B triangles. Make 13 and label these Unit 2.

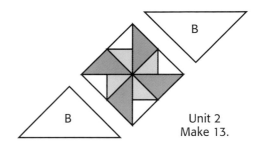

Unit 2
Make 13.

6. With right sides together, align one long raw edge of a 5½" × 9" rectangle to the left raw edge of each Unit 1. Pin, stitch, and press toward the rectangle. Make 2.

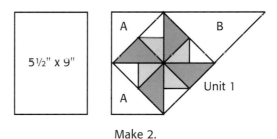

Make 2.

7. Arrange, then sew the 13 Unit 2 segments as shown in the first diagram below. Finish each end of the row with a Unit 1 segment to make a 15-block pieced bumper panel. Press.

8. Place the 2" × 42" accent border strips right sides together and sew them end to end to make one long continuous strip. From this strip, cut 2 strips, each 2" × 138", for the top and bottom accent borders.

9. Place the top and bottom accent border strips right sides together with the top and bottom edges of the pieced panel. Pin, stitch, and press the seams toward the border.

Finishing the Bumper Pad

1. Use the 2¼"-wide strips to construct 12 ties (see "Ties" on page 18).

2. Use the 3½" × 42" strips to construct a single long ruffle (see "Ruffles" on page 20).

3. Refer to the general instructions to add the ruffle and ties and to finish the bumper pad (see "Bumper Pad" on page 20). Notice in the second diagram below that the ruffle runs along only the top edge of the bumper pad, while the ties are along the top and bottom edges.

4. Quilt as desired (see "Quilting" on page 16). You might quilt beside the seam allowances (in-the-ditch) between the blocks and around the pinwheel triangles, and/or add any motifs you wish in the setting triangles.

Unit 1   Unit 1

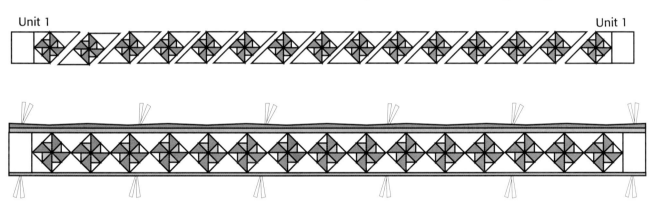

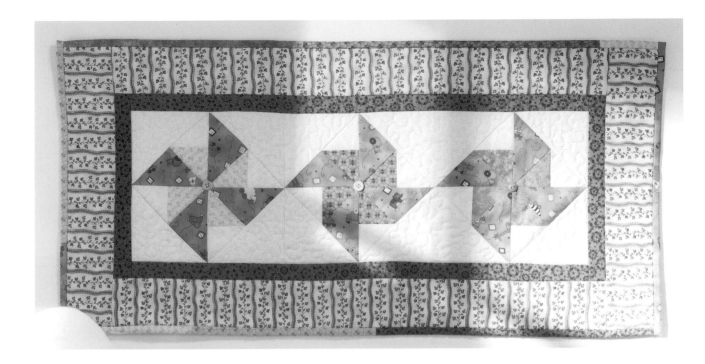

BRIGHT AND SHINING PINWHEELS WALL HANGING

Finished Quilt Size: 15½" × 32½"
Finished Block Size: 6"

Materials: (42"-wide fabric)

⅜ yd. light print or solid for background and setting triangles (A, B)

¼ yd. *each* of 3 different medium prints and/or solids for small pinwheel triangles*

¼ yd. dark print or solid for large pinwheel triangles*

¼ yd. dark contrasting print or solid for accent border

⅜ yd. bright print for outer border

⅝ yd. fabric for backing

⅜ yd. total assorted scraps for scrappy binding

20" × 36" rectangle of batting

Three 1"-diameter decorative buttons (optional)

*Or use scraps.

Cutting

From the light print or solid, cut:

2 squares, each 5¼" × 5¼", for end setting triangles (A)

1 square, 9¾" × 9¾", for setting triangles (B)

3 squares, each 4¼" × 4¼", for block backgrounds

From *each* of the 3 medium fabrics, cut:

1 square, 4¼" × 4¼", for small pinwheels

From the dark print or solid, cut:

6 squares, each 3⅞" × 3⅞", for large pinwheels

From the dark contrasting print or solid, cut:

2 strips, each 1½" × 25½", for top and bottom accent border

2 strips, each 1½" × 10½", for side accent border

From the bright print, cut:

2 strips, each 3" × 27½", for top and bottom outer border

2 strips, each 3" × 15½", for side outer border

From the backing fabric, cut:

1 rectangle, 20" × 36"

From the assorted scraps, cut:

2½"-wide strips to make a continuous strip length of 110" for binding

Assembling the Quilt Top

You will need 3 basic Pinwheel blocks for the Bright and Shining Pinwheels wall hanging.

1. Referring to "The Basic Pinwheel Block" on page 50, use the 4¼" light and medium squares and the 3⅞" dark squares to make a total of 3 Pinwheel blocks.

2. Cut each of the 5¼" squares on the diagonal in one direction to make a total of 4 end-setting triangles, 2 from each square. Label these A.

3. Cut the 9¾" square on the diagonal in both directions to make a total of 4 setting triangles. Label these B.

4. With right sides together, pin and sew the long diagonal side of an A triangle to 2 adjacent sides of a Pinwheel block as shown. Press toward the A triangles. With right sides together, pin and sew the short side of a B triangle to the Pinwheel block as shown. Press toward the B triangle. Make 2 and label these Unit 1.

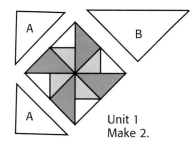

Unit 1
Make 2.

5. With right sides together, pin and sew the short side of a B triangle to opposite sides of a Pinwheel block as shown. Press toward the B triangle. Make 1 and label it Unit 2.

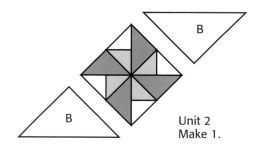

Unit 2
Make 1.

6. Arrange, pin, and sew a Unit 1 segment to either side of a Unit 2 segment as shown to make a 3-block pieced strip.

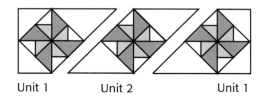

Unit 1   Unit 2   Unit 1

7. **Note:** For this project, the top and bottom borders are added first.

   Place the top and bottom accent border strips right sides together with the long top and bottom raw edges of the quilt. Pin, then sew the border strips to the quilt. Press the seam allowances toward the border. Repeat to add the side accent border strips, then the top, bottom, and side outer border strips to the quilt top (see "Adding Borders" on page 13).

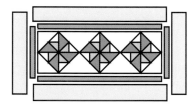

Finishing the Quilt

1. Layer the backing, batting, and quilt top for basting and baste the 3 layers (see "Assembling the Layers" on page 15).

2. Quilt as desired (see "Quilting" on page 16).

3. Bind with the 2½" × 110" scrappy binding strip to finish (see "French Binding" on page 16).

4. *If the wall hanging will be out of the child's reach,* sew buttons to the center of the pinwheels.

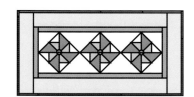

BRIGHT AND SHINING PINWHEELS HEADBOARD

Finished Headboard Size: 27" × 20"
Finished Block Size: 6"

Materials: (42"-wide fabric)

¼ yd. light print or solid for block backgrounds
¼ yd. *each* of 5 different medium prints and/or solids for small pinwheels
¼ yd. dark print or solid for large pinwheels
⅜ yd. medium green subtle print or solid for setting triangles (A)
⅜ yd. purple print for background
Assorted scraps to total ¼ yd. for ties

½ yd. coordinating print for ruffle
⅞ yd. fabric for backing
30" × 30" square of high-loft, bonded batting

Cutting

From the light print or solid, cut:
    5 squares, each 4¼" × 4¼", for block backgrounds
From *each* of the 5 medium fabrics, cut:
    1 square, 4¼" × 4¼", for small pinwheels
From the dark print or solid, cut:
    10 squares, each 3⅞" × 3⅞", for large pinwheels
From the medium green print or solid, cut:
    10 squares, each 5¼" × 5¼", for setting triangles (A)

From the purple print, cut:
    2 strips, each 4¾" × 9", for background
    1 strip, 4½" × 26", for background
From the assorted scraps, cut:
    5 strips *total*, each 2¼" × 20", for ties
From the coordinating print, cut:
    4 strips, each 3½"× 42", for ruffle
From the backing fabric, cut:
    1 square, 30" × 30"

Constructing the Headboard Panel

You will need 5 basic Pinwheel blocks for the Bright and Shining Pinwheels Headboard.

1. Referring to "The Basic Pinwheel Block" on page 50, use the 4¼" light and medium squares and the 3⅞" dark squares to make a total of 5 Pinwheel blocks.
2. Cut each of the 5¼" green squares once on the diagonal to make a total of 20 setting triangles, 2 from each square. Label these A.
3. With rights sides together and raw edges aligned, pin and sew the long diagonal edge of an A triangle to each side of a Pinwheel block. Press the seams toward the A triangles and square the blocks to 9".

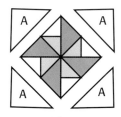

Make 5.

4. Arrange the 5 Pinwheel blocks, the 2 purple 4¾" × 9" strips, and the purple 4½" × 26" strip in 3 horizontal rows as shown in the upper right diagram. For Row 2, pin and sew the 2 Pinwheel blocks together, then sew to the long edge of a purple strip to finish each end of the row. For Row 3, pin and sew the 3 Pinwheel blocks to make a row. Whenever possible, press seams so they will oppose

matching seams when the rows are joined (see "Machine Piecing" on page 8).

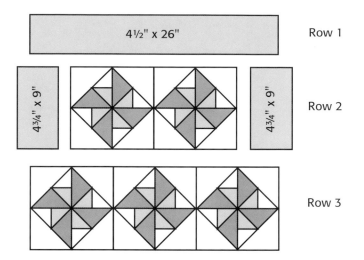

5. With right sides together and long raw edges aligned, pin, then sew the 3 rows to form the headboard panel. Press as desired.

Finishing the Headboard

1. Use the 2¼"-wide strips to construct 5 ties (see "Ties" on page 18).
2. Use the 3½" × 42" strips to construct a single long ruffle (see "Ruffles" on page 18).
3. Refer to the general instructions to add the ruffle and ties and to finish the headboard (see "Headboard" on page 20). Notice that the ruffle runs along only the top curved edge of the headboard. Position the ties as shown.
4. Quilt as desired (see "Quilting" on page 16).

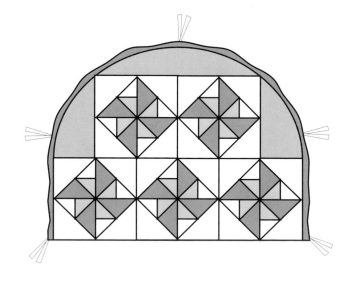

 # BRIGHT AND SHINING PINWHEELS VALANCE

Finished Valance Size: 67½" × 11½"
Finished Block Size: 6"

Materials: (42"-wide fabric)

¼ yd. light print or solid for block backgrounds
¼ yd. each of 5 different medium prints and/or solids for small pinwheels
¼ yd. dark print or solid for large pinwheels
⅝ yd. medium green subtle print or solid for setting triangles (A), sashes, and side borders
1 yd. purple print for lining and top and bottom border
Assorted scraps to total ¼ yd. for scrappy tabs
Twelve ½"-diameter decorative buttons

Cutting

From the light print or solid, cut:
   5 squares, each 4¼" × 4¼", for block backgrounds
From *each* of the 5 medium fabrics, cut:
   1 square, 4¼" × 4¼", for small pinwheels
From the dark print or solid, cut:
   10 squares, each 3⅞" × 3⅞", for large pinwheels
From the medium green print or solid, cut:
   10 squares, each 5¼" × 5¼", for setting triangles (A)
   4 strips, each 5½" × 9", for sashing
   2 rectangles, each 3" × 9", for side border
From the purple print, cut:
   2 strips, each 12" × 42", for lining
   4 strips, each 2" × 42", for top and bottom border
From the assorted scraps, cut:
   12 strips *total*, each 3" × 6", for tabs

Assembling the Valance Panel

You will need 5 basic Pinwheel blocks for the Bright and Shining Pinwheels Valance.

1. Referring to "The Basic Pinwheel Block" on page 50, use the 4¼" light and medium squares and the 3⅞" dark squares to make a total of 5 Pinwheel blocks.

2. Cut each of the 5¼" green squares once on the diagonal to make a total of 20 setting triangles, 2 from each square. Label these A.

3. With rights sides together and raw edges aligned, pin and sew the long diagonal edge of an A triangle to each side of a Pinwheel block. Press the seams toward the A triangles and square the blocks to 9".

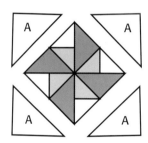

Make 5.

4. Arrange, then sew the blocks together as shown in the first diagram below. Place a 5½" × 9" green sashing strip between the blocks and a 3" × 9" green side border strip at either end of the panel. Press all seams toward the green strips. Refer to the project photo on

page 59 and the second diagram below for additional guidance.

5. Place two 2" × 42" purple border strips right sides together and sew them end to end to make 2 identical strips. Measure the valance across its horizontal center and cut the 2 long strips to this length for the top and bottom borders. Repeat to pair and trim the two 12" × 42" lining strips. Set the lining panel aside for now.

6. Place the top and bottom border strips right sides together with the top and bottom raw edges of the panel; pin and sew (see "Adding Borders" on page 13). Press toward the border.

Lining and Finishing the Valance

1. Use the 3" × 6" strips to make 12 tabs (see "Tabs" on page 19).

2. Use the 12"-wide lining strip to line the valance (see "Valance Lining and Finishing" on page 23).

3. Topstitch with a ¼" seam all around the outside edge of the valance.

4. Quilt as desired (see "Quilting" on page 16).

5. Bring the tabs to the front side of the valance and secure in place with decorative buttons.

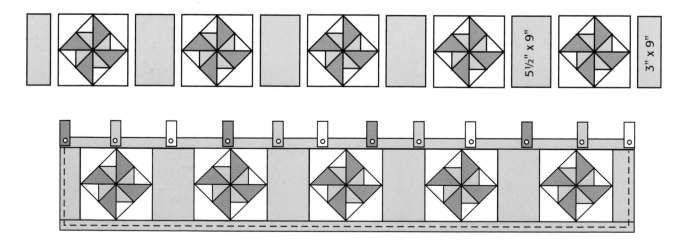

BRIGHT AND SHINING PINWHEELS DUST RUFFLE

Finished Mattress Base: 27" × 52"
Finished Drop: 16"

Materials: (42"-wide fabric)

1⅝ yds. muslin or a flat crib sheet for mattress base
2¼ yds. bright print for ruffle
1⅝ yds. coordinating medium print for bottom border

Cutting

Note: Adjust cutting instructions as needed to match crib measurements (see "Dust Ruffle" on page 22). Seam allowances are ¼" wide.

From the muslin or flat crib sheet, cut:
   1 panel, 28" × 53", for mattress base
From the bright print, cut:
   6 strips, each 12½" × 42", for ruffle
From the coordinating medium print, cut:
   6 strips, each 9" × 42", for bottom border

Constructing the Dust Ruffle

Refer to "Dust Ruffle" on page 22 to construct the basic dust ruffle. Use the 12¼"-wide strips for the ruffle, and the 9"-wide strips for the bottom border. Refer to the project photo above as needed.

BRIGHT AND SHINING PINWHEELS CRIB QUILT

Finished Quilt Size: 38" × 50" (plus ruffle)
Finished Block Size: 6"

Materials: (42"-wide fabric)

1⅝ yds. light subtle print or solid for block backgrounds, setting triangles (A, B), and inner and outer borders
¼ yd. *each* of 5 different medium prints and/or solids for small pinwheels
⅔ yd. dark print or solid for large pinwheels
¼ yd. bright green print for accent border
1 yd. total assorted fabrics for scrappy ruffle
1⅝ yds. fabric for backing
Crib-size batting (45" × 60")

Cutting

From the light print or solid, cut:
    3 strips, each 4½" × 42", for side outer borders
    2 strips, each 4½" × 38½", for top and bottom outer border
    2 strips, each 4¼" × 26", for side inner border
    2 strips, each 1¾" × 16½", for top and bottom inner border
    2 squares, each 5¼" × 5¼", for end-setting triangles (A)
    1 square, 9¾" × 9¾", for setting triangles (B)
    23 squares, each 4¼" × 4¼", for block backgrounds
From the 5 medium fabrics, cut:
    23 squares *total*, each 4¼" × 4¼", for small pinwheels
From the dark print or solid, cut:
    46 squares, each 3⅞" × 3⅞", for large pinwheels

From the bright green print, cut:
    2 strips, each 1½" × 28½", for side accent borders
    2 strips, each 1½" × 18½", for top and bottom accent borders
From the assorted fabrics, cut:
    4½"-wide strips to total 264" for the scrappy ruffle
From the backing fabric, cut:
    1 rectangle, 42" × 54"

Assembling the Quilt Top

You will need 23 basic Pinwheel blocks for the Bright and Shining Pinwheels Crib Quilt.

1. Referring to "The Basic Pinwheel Block" on page 50, use the 4¼" light and medium squares and the 3⅞" dark squares to make a total of 23 Pinwheel blocks.

2. Cut each of the 5¼" squares on the diagonal in one direction to make a total of 4 end-setting triangles, 2 from each square. Label these A.

3. Cut the 9¾" square on the diagonal in both directions to make a total of 4 setting triangles. Label these B.

4. With right sides together, pin and sew the long diagonal side of an A triangle to 2 adjacent sides of a Pinwheel block as shown. Press toward the A triangles. With right sides together, pin and sew the short side of a B triangle to the Pinwheel block as shown. Press toward the B triangle. Make 2 and label these Unit 1.

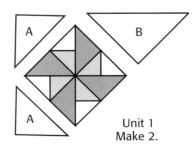

Unit 1
Make 2.

5. With right sides together, pin and sew the short side of a B triangle to opposite sides of a Pinwheel block as shown. Press toward the B triangles. Make 1 and label it Unit 2.

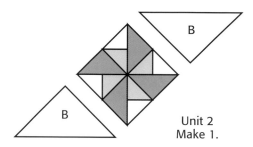

Unit 2
Make 1.

6. Arrange, pin, and sew a Unit 1 segment to either side of a Unit 2 segment as shown to make a 3-block pieced strip for the center of the quilt.

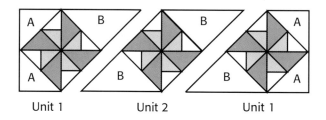

Unit 1   Unit 2   Unit 1

7. With right sides together and long raw edges aligned, pin and sew a 4¼" × 26" side inner border strip to each long side of the pieced center. Repeat to add 1¾" × 16½" top and bottom inner border strips to the top and bottom edges of the quilt.

8. Repeat the process described in step 7 to add the 1½" × 28½" side and 1½" × 18½" top and bottom accent border strips to the quilt.

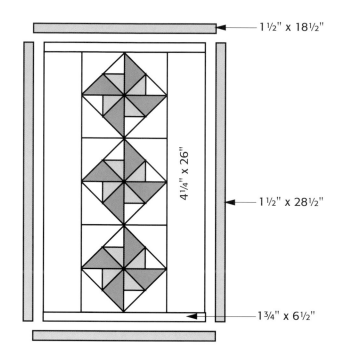

1½" x 18½"

4¼" x 26"

1½" x 28½"

1¾" x 6½"

69. Use the remaining Pinwheel blocks to make 4 rows of 5 Pinwheel blocks each.

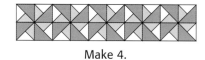

Make 4.

10. Place a Pinwheel side border strip right sides together with each side edge of the quilt top, matching the midpoints and ends. Pin generously and sew the border strips to the quilt, easing as necessary (see "Machine Piecing" on page 8). Press the seams toward the quilt center. Repeat to add the remaining Pinwheel strips to the top and bottom edges of the quilt.

11. Piece the 4½" × 42" border strips end to end to make one long continuous strip. Cut the strip into two 4½" × 42½" side borders. Repeat the procedure described in step 7 to add the 4½" × 42½" side outer border strips and the 4½" × 38½" top and bottom outer border strips to the quilt top.

Finishing the Quilt

1. Use the 4½"-wide scrappy strips to construct a ruffle (see "Ruffles" on page 18).
2. Use the easy-turn method to finish the quilt (see "Easy-Turn Finishing" on page 17). Make gentle curves around each corner as you are basting and sewing the ruffle to the quilt top. Refer to the quilt photo on page 62 and the diagram below for additional guidance.
3. Quilt as desired (see "Quilting" on page 16).
4. Finish the quilt by topstitching around the outer perimeter of the quilt, ¼" from the outside edge.

BRIGHT AND SHINING PINWHEELS PILLOWS

SMALL PILLOW

Finished Project and Block Size: 6" × 6" (plus ruffle)

Materials (42"-wide fabric) and Cutting

2 squares, each 4¼" × 4¼" (1 light for background, 1 medium for small pinwheel)

1 dark square, 3⅞" × 3⅞", for large pinwheel

1 square, 6½" × 6½", for backing

4½"-wide assorted strips to total 50" (approximately ⅜ yd.) for scrappy ruffle

6½" × 6½" square of batting

Small bag of polyester fiberfill or 6" pillow form

Constructing the Pillow

1. Referring to "The Basic Pinwheel Block" on page 50, use the 4¼" light and medium squares and the 3⅞" dark square to make 1 Pinwheel block.

2. Use the 4½"-wide assorted strips to construct a single long ruffle (see "Ruffles" on page 18).

3. Finish as directed in the general instructions (see "Pillow Finishing" on page 23).

LARGE PILLOW

Finished Project Size: 12" × 12" (plus ruffle)
Finished Block Size: 6"

Materials (42"-wide fabric) and Cutting

2 squares, each 4¼" × 4¼" (1 light for background, 1 medium for small pinwheel)

1 dark square, 3⅞" × 3⅞", for large pinwheel

2 strips, each 3½" × 6½", medium green print for side borders

2 strips, each 3½" × 12½", medium green print for top and bottom borders

1 square, 12½" × 12½", for backing

4½"-wide assorted strips to total 88" (approximately ½ yd.) for scrappy ruffle

12½" × 12½" square of batting

Small bag of polyester fiberfill or 12" pillow form

Constructing the Pillow

1. Referring to "The Basic Pinwheel Block" on page 50, use the 4¼" light and medium squares and the 3⅞" dark square to make 1 Pinwheel block.

2. With rights sides together, align the long raw edges of the side border strips with 2 sides of the Pinwheel block. Pin, sew, and press the seams toward the border. Repeat to add the top and bottom border strips to the remaining sides of the Pinwheel block.

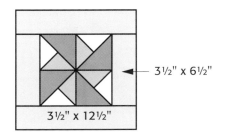

3½" x 6½"

3½" x 12½"

3. Use the 4½"-wide assorted strips to construct a single long ruffle (see "Ruffles" on page 18).

4. Finish as directed in the general instructions (see "Pillow Finishing" on page 23).

 ## BRIGHT AND SHINING PINWHEELS DECORATION

Instructions are for one decorative pinwheel made from fabric scraps.

Materials

2 squares, each 8½" × 8½" (1 *each* from 2 different contrasting prints or solids)

8½" square of fusible web

1 piece of ⅜"-diameter dowel, approximately 18" long

One ½"-diameter decorative button *or* 1"-diameter Yo-yo flower

Hot glue gun

Assembling the Pinwheel

1. Using the fusible web, follow the manufacturer's instructions to fuse the 2 fabric squares, wrong sides together. Trim the fused square to 8" × 8".

2. Draw an **X** from corner to corner on one side of the fused fabric square as shown.

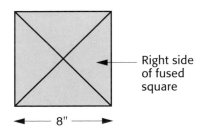

Right side of fused square

8"

3. From each corner, cut 3" toward the center of the square, directly on the drawn line.

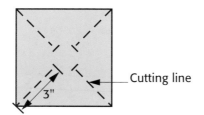

Cutting line

3"

4. Fold every other corner to the center and stitch in place.

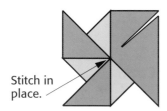

Stitch in place.

5. *If the pinwheel will be out of the child's reach*, hot glue or sew a Yo-yo flower or decorative button to the center of the pinwheel. Hot glue the pinwheel to the dowel.

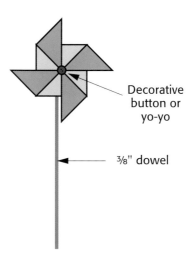

Decorative button or yo-yo

⅜" dowel

 ## BRIGHT AND SHINING PINWHEELS PAPIER-MÂCHÉ BOX

Materials

One 8"-square papier-mâché box

Assorted scraps to cover the box (approximately ⅝ yd.)

2 squares, each 8½" × 8½" (1 *each* from 2 different contrasting prints or solids)

1 square, 8½" × 8½", of fusible web

1 square, 8" × 8", of black felt

One 1"-diameter Yo-yo flower

Fray Check

1 sheet of PEELnSTICK (double-sided adhesive)

Hot glue gun

Decorating the Box

1. Refer to the instructions for the Bright and Shining Pinwheels Decoration, steps 1–4, on pages 67–68 to make a 3-dimensional pinwheel.

2. Measure the height and total width of the box sides and add 1" to each measurement. Cut the scrap fabric to this measurement. Apply Fray Check to the cut edges.

3. Cover the outside of the box with the PEELnSTICK.

4. Beginning at the top edge, with fabric and box edges even, adhere the fabric to the box. Overlap the ends and turn the raw edge under to finish the edges. Overlap 1" around the bottom edge and fuse. Cover the bottom of the box with the 8" square of black felt.

5. Measure and cut the fabric to cover the box lid.

6. Cut and fuse double-sided adhesive strips for the sides of the lid, then for the top.

7. Make a dot in the center of both the lid and the fabric with a straight pin.

8. Match the center dots of the fabric and the box lid; adhere the fabric to the lid, smoothing wrinkles as you go.

9. Fuse the pinwheel to the center of the lid. Hot glue the Yo-yo to the pinwheel center. If necessary, trim the pinwheel to fit the size of the box.

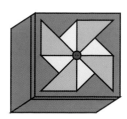

One Little Duck

Pinwheel blocks in a palette of cream, tan, yellow, and blue prove just right for a baby boy's or girl's nursery. The star of the collection is "One Little Duck," appliquéd on both the headboard and wall hanging. The crib quilt and dust ruffle with tulle overlay are appliquéd with random numbers and letters. A matching pillow, window valance, and utility bag complete the nursery decor.

ONE LITTLE DUCK BUMPER PAD

Finished Project Size: 137½" × 11½"
Finished Block Size: 6"

The bumper pad for One Little Duck is constructed in exactly the same manner as the Bright and Shining Pinwheels Bumper Pad. Only the colors are different. Refer to the instructions on pages 52–54 to complete the bumper pad. Substitute cream, yellow, tan, and blue fabrics as shown in the photo below for the brights used in the Pinwheel example.

🦆 ONE LITTLE DUCK WALL HANGING

Finished Quilt Size: 24" × 31"
Finished Block Size: 6"

Materials: (42"-wide fabric)

³/₈ yd. cream subtle print or solid for block backgrounds

¼ yd. *each* of 5 different medium yellow and tan prints and/or solids for small pinwheels

½ yd. dark blue print or solid for large pinwheels

½ yd. light subtle print or solid for appliqué background

⅓ yd. medium tan print for duck appliqué*

Assorted scraps to total ⅛ yd. for beak, feet, and letter appliqués

¼ yd. contrasting subtle print or solid for accent border

1 yd. fabric for backing

³/₈ yd. fabric for binding

27" × 34" piece of batting

*Or use scraps

Fourteen ½"-diameter decorative buttons (optional)

½ yd. lightweight fusible web

Assorted skeins of DMC embroidery floss to match appliqué fabrics

Cutting

From the cream print or solid, cut:
  14 squares, each 4¼" × 4¼", for block backgrounds
From the 5 medium yellow and tan fabrics, cut:
  14 squares *total*, each 4¼" × 4¼", for small pinwheels
From the dark blue print or solid, cut:
  28 squares, each 3⅞" × 3⅞", for large pinwheels
From the light print or solid, cut:
  1 panel, 11½" × 17½", for appliqué background
From the contrasting print or solid, cut:
  2 strips, each 1" × 17½", for side border
  2 strips, each 1" × 12½", for top and bottom border
From the backing fabric, cut:
  1 rectangle, 28" × 34"
From the binding fabric, cut:
  3 strips, each 2½" × 42"

Assembling the Center Panel

1. Use the pattern pieces on pages 136–138 to trace appliqué pieces A through G. Refer to the instructions for "Fusible-Web Appliqué" on page 10 to prepare, cut, fuse, and stitch the appliqués in place on the background panel. If you prefer, you may hand appliqué the motifs (see "Hand Appliqué" on page 11). You'll need to cut 1 of each appliqué piece. Refer to the upper right diagram, the wall hanging photo on page 73, and the diagrams on page 75 for guidance in positioning the pieces.

2. Use the DMC floss to make an eye for the duck, outline the wing, and add any other details as desired (see "Embroidery Stitches" on page 12).

3. With right sides together, align the long raw edges, pin, and sew a 1" × 17½" side border strip to each long side of the center panel. Repeat to add 1" × 12½" top and bottom border strips to the short top and bottom edges of the panel. Press the seams toward the center panel.

Assembling the Pinwheel Borders

You will need 14 basic Pinwheel blocks for the pieced border on the One Little Duck Wall Hanging.

1. Referring to "The Basic Pinwheel Block" on page 50, use the 4¼" cream, yellow, and tan squares and the 3⅞" dark blue squares to make 14 Pinwheel blocks.

2. With right sides together, pin and sew 3 Pinwheel blocks in a row as shown. Make 2 and label these Border 1.

3. With right sides together, pin and sew 4 Pinwheel blocks in a row as shown. Make 2 and label these Border 2.

Border 1
Make 2.

Border 2
Make 2.

4. With right sides together and long raw edges aligned, pin and sew a Border 1 strip to each long side of the quilt top. Repeat to add Border 2 strips to the top and bottom edges of the quilt top. Press the seams toward the border.

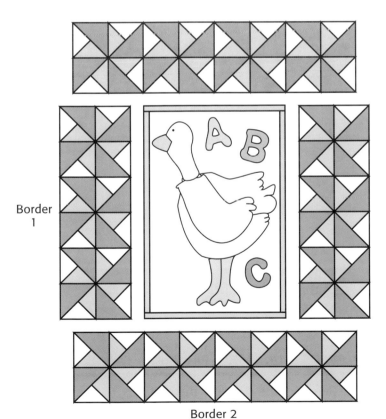

Border 1

Border 2

Finishing the Quilt

1. Layer the backing, batting, and quilt top for basting and baste the 3 layers (see "Assembling the Layers" on page 15).

2. Quilt as desired (see "Quilting" on page 16).

3. Use the 2½" × 42" strips to make binding and bind to finish (see "French Binding" on page 16).

4. *If the wall hanging will be out of the child's reach, sew the buttons to the pinwheel centers.*

 ## ONE LITTLE DUCK
HEADBOARD

Finished Headboard Size: 27" × 20"

Materials: (42"-wide fabric)

⅞ yd. light subtle print or solid for background

⅓ yd. medium tan print for duck appliqué*

Assorted scraps to total ⅛ yd. for feet, beak, letter, and number appliqués

¼ yd. coordinating prints or solids for ties*

½ yd. contrasting blue print for ruffle

⅞ yd. fabric for backing

30" × 30" square of high-loft, bonded batting

½ yd. lightweight fusible web

Assorted skeins of DMC embroidery floss to match appliqué fabrics

*Or use scraps.

Cutting

From the light print or solid, cut:
    1 square, 30" × 30", for background
From the coordinating prints or solids, cut
    5 strips, each 2¼" × 20", for ties
From the contrasting blue print, cut:
    4 strips, each 3½" × 42", for ruffle
From the backing fabric, cut:
    1 square, 30" × 30"

Constructing the Headboard Panel

1. Refer to the general instructions to make a full-size template for the headboard (see "Headboard," step 1, page 20).

2. Center the headboard template on the 30" × 30" light background square. Trace around the template, remove it, and machine baste ⅛" inside the traced line. Cut on the traced line.

3. Use the pattern pieces on pages 136–138 to trace appliqué pieces A through J. Refer to the instructions for "Fusible-Web Appliqué" on page 10 to prepare, cut, fuse, and stitch the appliqués in place on the background panel. You'll need to cut 1 of each appliqué piece. Refer to the diagram on page 74, the project photo on page 76, and the diagram below for guidance in positioning the pieces.

4. Use the DMC floss to embroider an eye for the duck, outline the wing, and add any other details as desired (see "Embroidery Stitches" on page 12).

Finishing the Headboard

1. Use the 2¼"-wide strips to construct 5 ties (see "Ties" on page 18).

2. Use the 3½" × 12" strips to construct a single long ruffle (see "Ruffles" on page 18).

3. Refer to the general instructions to add the ruffle and ties and to finish the headboard (see "Headboard" on page 20). Notice that the ruffle runs along only the top curved edge of the headboard. Position the ties as shown.

4. Quilt as desired (see "Quilting" on page 16).

ONE LITTLE DUCK VALANCE

Finished Valance Size: 68" × 13"
Finished Block Size: 6"

Materials: (42"-wide fabric)

¼ yd. cream subtle print or solid for block backgrounds
¼ yd. *each* of 5 different medium yellow and tan prints and/or solids for small pinwheels
⅜ yd. dark blue print or solid for large pinwheels
½ yd. medium yellow print or solid for setting triangles (A, B)
⅜ yd. contrasting print or solid for accent border
¼ yd. dark blue print or solid for tabs*
⅝ yd. contrasting blue print for ruffle
⅞ yd. fabric for lining
Twelve ¼"-diameter decorative buttons

*Or use scraps.

Cutting

From the cream print or solid, cut:
    8 squares, each 4¼" × 4¼", for block backgrounds
From the 5 medium yellow and tan fabrics, cut:
    8 squares *total*, each 4¼" × 4¼", for small pinwheels
From the dark blue print or solid, cut:
    16 squares, each 3⅞" × 3⅞", for large pinwheels
From the medium yellow print or solid, cut:
    2 squares, each 5¼" × 5¼", for end setting triangles (A)
    4 squares, each 9¾" × 9¾", for setting triangles (B)
From the contrasting print or solid, cut:
    4 strips, each 2" × 42", for border
From the dark blue print or solid, cut:
    12 strips, each 3" × 6", for tabs
From the contrasting blue print, cut:
    5 strips, each 3½" × 42", for ruffle

From the lining fabric, cut:

2 strips, each 13½" × 42"

Assembling the Valance Panel

You will need 8 basic Pinwheel blocks for the One Little Duck Valance.

1. Referring to "The Basic Pinwheel Block" on page 50, use the 4¼" cream, yellow, and tan squares and the 3⅞" dark blue squares to make 8 Pinwheel blocks.

2. Cut each of the 5¼" squares on the diagonal in one direction to make a total of 4 end-setting triangles, 2 from each square. Label these A.

3. Cut each of the 9¾" squares on the diagonal in both directions to make a total of 16 setting triangles. Label these B.

4. With right sides together, pin and sew the long diagonal side of an A triangle to 2 adjacent sides of a Pinwheel block as shown. Press toward the A triangles. With right sides

together, pin and sew the short side of a B triangle to the Pinwheel block as shown. Press toward the B triangle. Make 2 and label these Unit 1.

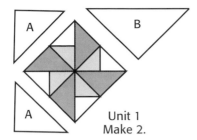

Unit 1
Make 2.

5. With right sides together, pin and sew the short side of a B triangle to opposite sides of a Pinwheel block as shown. Press toward the B triangles. Make 6 and label them Unit 2.

Note: You'll have 2 B triangles left over.

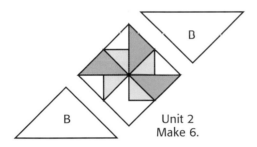

Unit 2
Make 6.

6. Arrange the units into a single horizontal row, then sew the units together as shown in the diagram.

Unit 1   Unit 2

Unit 1

7. Place two 2" × 42" accent border strips right sides together and sew them end to end to make 2 identical strips. Measure the valance across its horizontal center and cut the 2 long strips to this length for the top and bottom borders. Repeat to pair and trim the two 13½" × 42" lining strips. Set the lining panel aside for now.

8. Place the top and border strips right sides together with the top and bottom raw edges of the panel; pin and sew (see "Adding Borders" on page 13). Press toward the border.

Lining and Finishing the Valance

1. Use the 3" × 6" strips to make 12 tabs (see "Tabs" on page 19).
2. Use the 3½"-wide blue strips to construct a ruffle (see "Ruffles" on page 18). Pin the ruffle right sides together with the bottom edge of the pieced valance panel, matching the long raw edges.
3. Use the 13½"-wide lining panel to line the valance (see "Valance Lining and Finishing" on page 23).
4. Topstitch the top and bottom outside edges of the valance with a ¼"-wide seam allowance.
5. Quilt as desired (see "Quilting" on page 16).
6. Bring the tabs to the front side of the valance and secure in place with decorative buttons.

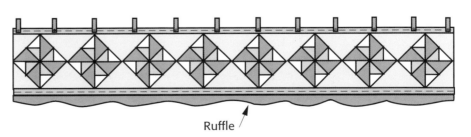

Ruffle

🦢 ONE LITTLE DUCK DUST RUFFLE

Finished Mattress Base: 27" × 52"
Finished Drop: 16"

Materials: (42"-wide fabric)

1⅝ yds. muslin or a flat crib sheet for mattress base

2⅜ yds. blue print for ruffle

3 yds. tulle for overlay

1¾ yds. yellow print for bottom border

¾ yd. lightweight fusible web

Assorted coordinating scraps to total ⅜ yd. for appliqués

Cutting

Note: Adjust cutting instructions as needed to match crib measurements (see "Dust Ruffle" on page 22). Seam allowances are ¼" wide.

From the muslin or flat crib sheet, cut:
　1 panel, 28" × 53", for mattress base
From the blue print, cut:
　6 strips, each 12½" × 42", for ruffle
From the tulle, cut:
　6 strips, each 17" × 42", for overlay
From the yellow print, cut:
　6 strips, each 9" × 42", for bottom border

Constructing the Dust Ruffle

1. Refer to "Dust Ruffle," steps 1–5, on page 22 to construct the basic dust ruffle. Use the 12½"-wide strips for the ruffle, and the 9"-wide strips for the bottom border. Refer to the project photo on page 80 as needed.

2. Use the pattern pieces on page 138 to trace appliqué pieces E through J. Refer to the instructions for "Fusible-Web Appliqué" on page 10 to prepare, cut, fuse, and stitch the appliqués in place on the bottom border ruffles. If you prefer, you may hand appliqué the motifs (see "Hand Appliqué" on page 11). You'll need to cut 6 of each appliqué piece. Refer to the diagram below for guidance in positioning 2 of each letter and number on the border for each side ruffle, and 1 of each letter and number on the border of the head and foot ruffles.

3. To construct the tulle overlay, repeat steps 1 and 2 in the general instructions for constructing a dust ruffle (see page 22). Hem the bottom edges with a double ¼"-wide seam.

4. Taper the corners of the mattress base with a double ½" diagonal fold and topstitch as shown in the diagram on page 22.

5. Place 1 side of the tulle overlay right sides together with 1 side of the mattress base, aligning the raw edges. Gather the tulle evenly to fit the mattress base; pin in place. Baste the tulle to the base with a ⅛"-wide seam allowance. Repeat to attach the other 3 overlays to the mattress base.

6. Refer to "Dust Ruffle," steps 7 and 8, on pages 22–23 to complete the dust ruffle.

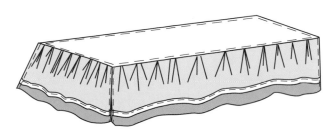

 ONE LITTLE DUCK CRIB QUILT

Finished Quilt Size: 39" × 53"
Finished Block Size: 6"

Materials: (42"-wide fabric)

½ yd. cream subtle print or solid for block backgrounds and corner squares

¼ yd. *each* of 5 different medium yellow and tan prints and/or solids for small pinwheels

⅔ yd. dark blue print or solid for large pinwheels

⅝ yd. dark tan subtle print or solid for sashing and accent border

⅞ yd. coordinating light print for outer border

Assorted coordinating scraps to total ⅜ yd. for appliqués

1½ yds. dark blue print for ruffle

1⅝ yds. fabric for backing

Crib-size batting (45" × 60")

⅝ yd. lightweight fusible web

Cutting

From the cream print or solid, cut:
    1 strip, 1½" × 42", for corner squares
    24 squares, each 4¼" × 4¼", for block backgrounds

From the 5 medium yellow and tan fabrics, cut:
    24 squares *total*, each 4¼" × 4¼", for small pinwheels

From the dark blue print or solid, cut:
    48 squares, each 3⅞" × 3⅞", for large pinwheels

From the dark tan print or solid, cut:
    7 strips, each 1½" × 42", for sashing
    2 strips, each 1½" × 41½", for side accent borders
    2 strips, each 1½" × 27", for top and bottom accent borders

From the coordinating light print, cut:
    5 strips, each 5½" × 42", for outer borders

From the dark blue print, cut:
  9 strips, each 5" × 42", for ruffle
From the backing fabric, cut:
  1 panel, 39½" × 53½"

Assembling the Quilt Top

You will need 24 basic Pinwheel blocks for the One Little Duck Crib Quilt.

1. Referring to "The Basic Pinwheel Block" on page 50, use the 4¼" cream, yellow, and tan squares and the 3⅞" dark blue squares to make 24 Pinwheel blocks.

2. Cut the 1½" × 42" tan sashing strips into 6½" segments. Cut a total of 38.

3. Lay out 6 horizontal rows of 4 blocks each to check for a pleasing balance. When you are satisfied, pin and sew the blocks into 6 rows, placing a 1½" × 6½" sashing strip between each block as shown. Press the seams toward the sashing.

Sashing strip

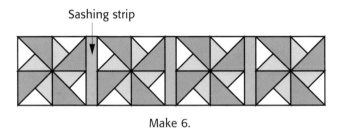

Make 6.

4. Crosscut the 1½" × 42" cream strip into 19 corner squares, each 1½" × 1½".

5. Lay 4 sashing strips end to end to make a long horizontal row. Place a 1½" corner square between each strip as shown. Pin and sew the squares and strips end to end. Press the seams toward the strips. Repeat to make a total of 5 pieced strips.

Corner square

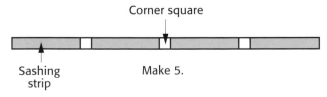

Sashing
strip   Make 5.

6. Lay out the 6 rows of Pinwheel blocks as shown, with a pieced strip separating the horizontal rows. With right sides together, raw edges aligned, and seams matched carefully, pin and sew the quilt top together, row by row (see "Machine Piecing" on page 8). Press the seams toward the pieced strips.

7. With right sides together and raw edges aligned, pin and sew a 1½" × 41½" side accent strip to each side of the quilt top. Press the seams toward the strips.

8. Sew a remaining corner square to each short end of the 1½" × 27½" top and bottom accent strips. Repeat the process described in step 7 to sew the pieced accent strips to the top and bottom edges of the quilt top.

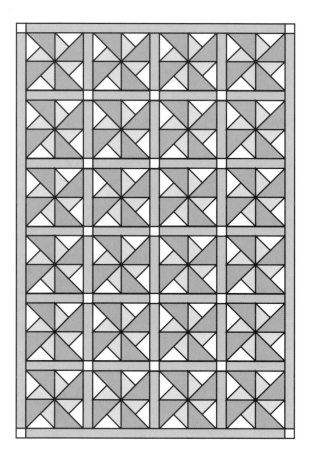

9. Sew the 5½" × 42" outer border strips together end to end. Measure the quilt top and cut the 5½"-wide strip into side, top, and bottom border strips to fit (see "Adding Borders" on page 13).

10. Use the pattern pieces on page 138 to trace appliqué pieces E through J. Refer to the instructions for "Fusible-Web Appliqué" on page 10 to prepare, cut, fuse, and stitch the appliqués in place on the border strips. If you prefer, you may hand appliqué the motifs (see "Hand Appliqué" on page 11). You'll need to cut 5 E, 6 each of F and G, and 4 each of H, I, and J. Refer to the quilt photo

on page 83 and the diagram below for guidance in positioning the appliqués.

11. With right sides together and raw edges aligned, pin and sew the side, then the top and bottom appliqué borders to the quilt (see "Adding Borders" on page 13). Press the seams toward the appliqué borders.

Finishing the Quilt

1. Use the 5"-wide blue strips to construct a ruffle (see "Ruffles" on page 18).

2. Use the easy-turn method to finish the quilt (see "Easy-Turn Finishing" on page 17). Make gentle curves around each corner as you are basting and sewing the ruffle to the quilt top. Sew with a ½"-wide seam allowance. Refer to the quilt photo on page 83 and the diagram below for additional guidance.

3. Quilt as desired (see "Quilting" on page 16).

4. Finish the quilt by topstitching around the outer perimeter of the quilt, ¼" from the outside edge.

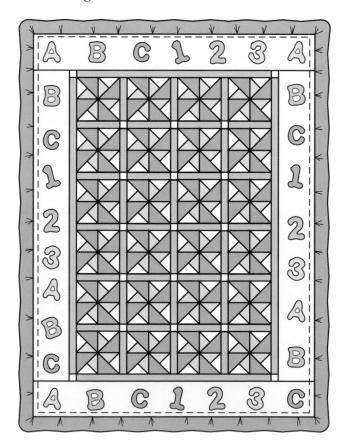

ONE LITTLE DUCK
PILLOW

Finished Pillow Size: 14½" (plus ruffle)
Finished Block Size: 6"

Materials (42"-wide fabric)
and Cutting

4 squares, each 4¼" × 4¼", cream subtle print or
solid for block backgrounds

4 squares *total*, each 4¼" × 4¼", of 4 different
yellow and tan prints for small pinwheels

8 squares, each 3⅞" × 3⅞", dark blue print for
large pinwheels

2 strips, each 1¾" × 12½", dark tan print or
solid for side border

2 strips, each 1¾" × 15", of *same* dark tan print
for top and bottom border (¼ yd. total)

1 square, 15" × 15", coordinating light print for
backing

3 strips, each 7" × 42", of *same* coordinating
light print for ruffle (1⅛ yds. total)

3 strips, each 7" × 42", of tulle for ruffle overlay
(¾ yd.)

1 square, 15" × 15", of cotton batting

Small bag of polyester fiberfill

Constructing the Pillow

You will need 4 basic Pinwheel blocks for the One Little Duck Pillow.

1. Referring to "The Basic Pinwheel Block" on page 50, use the 4¼" cream, yellow, and tan squares and the 3⅞" dark blue squares to make 4 Pinwheel blocks.

2. Arrange the Pinwheel blocks in 2 rows of 2 blocks each. With right sides together and raw edges aligned, pin and sew the blocks together. Press the center seam in opposing directions; pin and join the rows (see "Machine Piecing" on page 8).

3. With right sides together, pin and sew a 1¾" × 15" side border strip to 2 sides of the 4-block unit. Press toward the border. Repeat to add the 1¾" × 15" top and bottom border strips to the remaining sides of the unit.

4. Use the 7" × 42" light print strips to partially construct a ruffle (see "Ruffles," steps 1–2, page 18). Repeat with the 7" × 42" tulle strips. Lay the tulle ruffle over the light print ruffle and pin. Complete construction of this double ruffle (see "Ruffles," steps 3–6, page 18).

5. Finish as directed in the general instructions (see "Pillow Finishing" on page 23).

MOM'S UTILITY BAG

Finished Bag Size: 20" × 28" (approx.)

The sample bag and the accompanying instructions call for 12 *totally* scrappy basic Pinwheel blocks. Blocks from the other collections may be substituted with a few simple adjustments. The pieced blocks from the Sugar Bunny Crib Quilt may be substituted for pinwheels with no size adjustment. The Little Sailor's Dream quilt blocks are 5½", so you will need to adjust the sashing and the middle border. For another option, eliminate the pieced blocks entirely and adjust the fabric requirements to make a solid bag decorated with flower appliqués from the Baby's Secret Garden collection. The bag may be used for laundry, extra diapers, toys, or whatever Mom chooses.

Materials: (42"-wide fabric)

⅜ yd. light print for pinwheel backgrounds

⅜ yd. *total* assorted medium prints for small pinwheels

½ yd. *total* assorted dark prints for large pinwheels

⅛ yd. light print or solid for vertical sashing

¼ yd. medium print or solid for horizontal sashing

¾ yd. fabric of your choice for bag

⅞ yd. muslin for lining

20" × 42" piece of batting

1⅔ yds. cable cording for ¼-diameter drawstring

Fray Check

Cutting

From the light print, cut:
  12 squares, each 4¼" × 4¼", for block backgrounds
From the assorted medium prints, cut:
  12 squares *total*, each 4¼" × 4¼", for small pinwheels
From the assorted dark prints, cut:
  4 squares *total*, each 3⅞" × 3⅞", for large pinwheels
From the light sashing fabric, cut:
  12 strips, each ⅞" × 6½", for vertical sashing
From the medium sashing fabric, cut:
  3 strips, each 1½" × 38¾", for horizontal sashing
From the bag fabric, cut:
  1 panel, 18" × 38¾", for bag top
  1 strip, 6½" × 13⅛", for bag bottom
From the lining fabric, cut:
  1 panel, 23¼" × 38¾", for bag top
  1 strip, 6½" × 13⅛", for bag bottom

Constructing the Bag

1. Referring to "The Basic Pinwheel Block" on page 50, use the 4¼" light and medium squares and the 3⅞" dark squares to make 12 Pinwheel blocks.

2. Lay out 2 horizontal rows of 6 blocks each to check for a pleasing balance. When you are satisfied, pin and sew the blocks into rows, placing a ⅞" × 6½" vertical sashing strip between each block and ending each row as shown. Press the seams toward the blocks.

3. With right sides together and long raw edges aligned, pin and sew a 1½" × 38¾" horizontal sashing strip to the top edge of each row. Stitch the rows together as shown and finish the panel by adding the remaining 1½"-wide sashing strip to the bottom edge. Press seams toward the sashing.

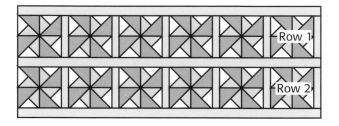

4. Layer the pieced panel on top of the batting and pin from the center out, smoothing wrinkles as you go. Quilt beside the seams (in-the-ditch) between the blocks and sashing or as desired (see "Quilting" on page 16). Trim the excess batting and press.

5. With right sides together, align the long raw edge of the top bag section with the top edge of the quilted panel. Pin and sew.

6. With right sides together, fold the bag in half so that the seams of the pieced panel meet. Pin and sew to create a tube; press the seam open.

7. Press the top raw edge under ¼". To find the placement for the buttonhole opening, measure 8½" down from the center at the top front edge and mark with a pin. To stabilize the buttonhole, place a 1" square of fabric on the wrong side of the bag at the pin and make a ½" buttonhole on the right side. Apply Fray Check to the buttonhole, allow to dry, and cut the opening.

8. Fold over the top of the bag 4½" to the inside and press.

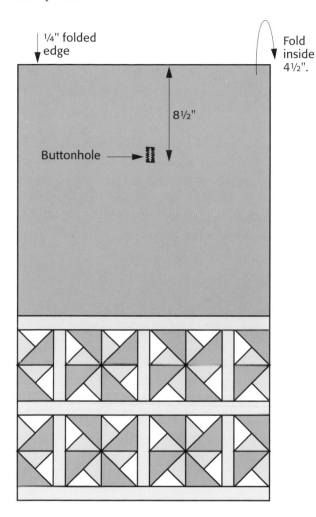

1/4" folded edge

Fold inside 4½".

8½"

Buttonhole

Attaching the Bag Bottom

1. Match the bottom back seam of the bag to the front to find the front center point. Mark the front center with a pin, then identify and mark the center points of each side of the bag.
2. Fold the 6½" × 13⅛" bag bottom in half lengthwise and mark the center points with pins. Open and refold in half crosswise to identify and mark the center points on the other 2 sides.
3. With right sides together, pin the bottom to the bag, matching the pin marks, and sew.

Lining and Finishing

1. Fold the bag lining right sides together, matching the 23¼" raw edges. Sew to create a tube and press the seam open.
2. Repeat steps 1–3, "Attaching the Bag Bottom" to attach the bag lining to the bottom lining; press.
3. With wrong sides together and back center seams matched, place the lining inside the bag. Overlap the top raw edge of the lining with the outer bag. Topstitch ¼" from the top edge through all layers.
4. Match the lining and the bag bottom seams; pin. Stitch beside the seam line (in-the ditch) on the bottom seams through all layers; press.
5. Measure 3¾" down from the top edge of the bag and stitch all around the bag through all layers.
6. Thread the cording through the buttonhole and casing, knot the ends.

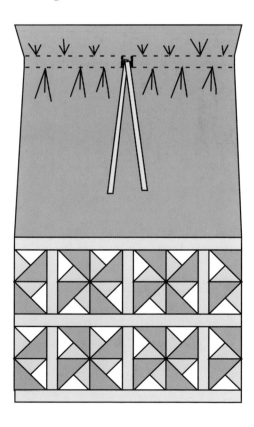

Sugar Bunny

Sugar Bunny

Soft, cuddly, and sweet—just like that baby girl! Sugar Bunny watches over her as she's snuggled in a soft, flannel pieced quilt of pinks, blues, and greens. Sugar Bunny herself is appliquéd on a pink flannel headboard backed with chenille and seems to be waiting for baby to come out and play. The matching dust ruffle is also made with flannel and chenille. Matching flannel pillows, bumper pad, wall hanging, and window valance complete the collection.

SUGAR BUNNY BUMPER PAD

Finished Bumper Pad Size: 137½" × 11½"
Finished Block Size: 6"

Materials: (42"-wide fabric)

¼ yd. *each* of light, medium, and dark print flannels in blue *and* green for pieced blocks*

⅞ yd. pink print flannel for setting triangles (A) and side panels

1 yd. yellow print flannel for top and bottom accent border and ties

⅞ yd. green print flannel for ruffle

12" × 138" panel of blue chenille for backing

12" × 138" panel of high-loft, bonded batting**

2½ yds. total of coordinating blue, green, and/or pink ⅛"-wide ribbon

*You should have a light, medium, and dark in each color. Use a total of 6 fabrics.
**Batting may be pieced.

Cutting

From *each* of the 6 blue and green flannels, cut:
 3 strips, each 1½" × 42", for pieced blocks
From the pink print flannel, cut:
 2 squares, each 5¼" × 5¼", for end setting triangles (A)
 7 squares, each 9¾" × 9¾", for setting triangles (B)
 2 strips, each 5½" × 9", for side border panels
From the yellow print flannel, cut:
 7 strips, each 2" × 42", for top and bottom accent borders
 12 strips, each 2¼" × 20", for ties
From the green print flannel, cut:
 8 strips, each 3½" × 42", for ruffle

Assembling the Bumper Panel

1. Arrange a light, medium, and dark 1½"-wide blue flannel strip to form a 3-strip set, placing the light strip in the center. With right sides together, pin and sew the strip set, pressing the seams in one direction. Make 3 identical blue strip sets.

2. Repeat step 1 to arrange and sew 3 identical 3-strip sets with the 1½"-wide green strips.

3. Measure the width of each strip set, including the seam allowance. (It should be 3½".) Cut each strip set into 3½" segments. You'll need a total of 28 blue segments and 32 green segments.

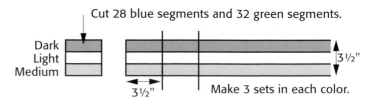

4. Sew 4 same-color segments together to make a block, rotating the segments as shown. The dark strips should appear in the center of the block to create a pinwheel effect. You'll have a total of 15 blocks, 7 blue and 8 green.

Make 7 blue and 8 green blocks.

5. Cut each of the 5¼" pink squares in half on the diagonal in one direction to make a total of 4 end setting triangles, 2 from each square. Label these A.

6. Cut each of the 9¾" squares on the diagonal in both directions to make a total of 28 setting triangles, 4 from each square. Label these B.

7. With right sides together, pin and sew the long diagonal side of an A triangle to 2 adjacent sides of a Pinwheel block as shown. Press toward the A triangles. With right sides together, pin and sew the short side of a B triangle to the Pinwheel block as shown. Press toward the B triangle. Make 2 and label these Unit 1.

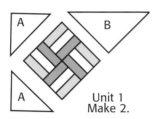

Unit 1
Make 2.

8. With right sides together, pin and sew the short side of a B triangle to opposite sides of a Pinwheel block as shown. Press toward the B triangles. Make 13 and label these Unit 2.

Note: You'll have 2 B triangles left over.

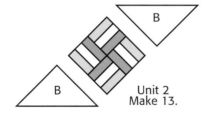

Unit 2
Make 13.

9. Use the pattern pieces on page 139 to trace appliqué pieces N and O. Refer to the instructions for "Fusible-Web Appliqué" on page 10 to prepare, cut, fuse, and stitch the appliqués in place on the bumper pad. If you prefer, you may hand appliqué the star motifs (see "Hand Appliqué" on page 11). You'll need to cut 4 each of N and O. "Stack" a pair of stars vertically down the center of each 5½" × 9" pink rectangle, spacing them evenly. Refer to the the diagram on page 95 for guidance in placing the appliqués.

10. With right sides together, align one long raw edge of a 5½" × 9" rectangle to the left raw edge of each Unit 1. Pin, stitch, and press toward the rectangle. Make 2.

11. Arrange, then sew the 13 Unit 2 segments as shown in the diagram below. Finish each end of the row with a Unit 1 segment to make a 15-block pieced bumper panel. Press.

12. Place the 2" × 42" border strips right sides together and sew them end to end to make one long continuous strip. From this strip, cut 2 strips, each 2" × 138", for the top and bottom accent borders.

Unit 2

Unit 1   Unit 1

13. Place the top and bottom accent borders right sides together with the top and bottom raw edges of the pieced panel. Pin, stitch, and press the seams toward the border strips.

Finishing the Bumper Pad

1. Use the 2¼"-wide strips to construct 12 ties (see "Ties" on page 18).
2. Use the 3½" × 42" strips to construct a single long ruffle (see "Ruffles" on page 18).

3. Refer to the general instructions to add the ruffle and ties and to finish the bumper pad (see "Bumper Pad" on page 20). Notice in the diagram below that the ruffle runs along only the top edge of the bumper pad, while the ties are along the top and bottom edges.
4. Quilt as desired (see "Quilting" on page 16). You might quilt beside the seam allowances (in-the-ditch) between the blocks and the strips and/or add any motifs you wish in the setting triangles.
5. Tack the midpoint of a 6" length of ⅛"-wide ribbon to the center of each pieced block and tie in a bow.

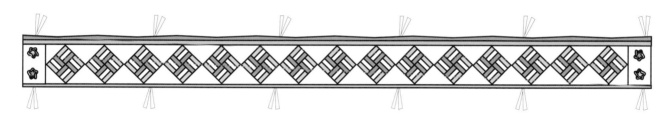

SUGAR BUNNY WALL HANGING

Finished Quilt Size: 22" × 27"

Materials: (42"-wide fabric)

½ yd. green subtle print or solid flannel for appliqué background

¼ yd. yellow subtle print or solid flannel for accent border

½ yd. green print flannel for outer border

⅛ yd. *each* of cream, pink, blue, and green prints for bunny, star, collar, and shoe appliqués

¼ yd. yellow print for dress appliqué

⅔ yd. fabric for backing

¼ yd. pink flannel for binding

25" × 30" rectangle of batting

1 skein each of pink and black DMC embroidery floss

Cutting

From the green print or solid flannel, cut:
    1 panel, 12½" × 17½", for appliqué background
From the yellow print or solid flannel, cut:
    2 strips, each 1½" × 17½", for side accent border
    2 strips, each 1½" × 14½", for top and bottom accent border
From the green print flannel, cut:
    2 strips, each 4½" × 19½", for side outer border
    2 strips, each 4½" × 22½", for top and bottom outer border
From the backing fabric, cut:
    1 piece, 26" × 31"
From the pink flannel, cut:
    3 strips, each 2½" × 42", for binding

Assembling the Quilt Top

1. Use the pattern pieces on pages 139–140 to trace appliqué pieces A through N. Refer to the instructions for "Fusible-Web Appliqué" on page 10 to prepare, cut, fuse, and stitch the appliqués in place on the background panel. If you prefer, you may hand appliqué the motifs (see "Hand Appliqué" on page 11). You'll need to cut 1 each of pieces A, C, C reversed, D, E, F, G, Ia, Ib, J, J reversed, K, L, and L reversed; 2 each of B and M; 3 of N; and 15 of H. Refer to the diagram below, the project photo on page 97, and the diagram on page 98 for guidance in positioning the pieces.

2. Embroider Sugar Bunny's facial features using 2 strands of floss. Use a satin stitch for the eyes (black) and nose (pink), and an outline stitch (black) for the mouth. Refer to the Appliqué Placement Diagram and the E pattern piece for guidance.

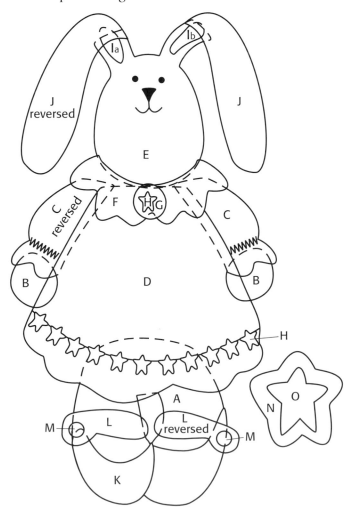

3. With right sides together and long raw edges aligned, pin and sew a 1½" × 17½" side accent border strip to each long side of the appliquéd center panel. Repeat to add 1½" × 14½" top and bottom accent border strips to the top and bottom edges of the panel (see "Adding Borders" on page 13).

4. Repeat the procedure described in step 3 to add a 4½" × 19½" side outer border strip to each side of the quilt top and 4½" × 22½" top and bottom outer border strips to the top and bottom edges.

Finishing the Quilt

1. Layer the backing, batting, and quilt top for basting and baste the 3 layers (see "Assembling the Layers" on page 15).

2. Quilt as desired (see "Quilting" on page 16).

3. Use the 2½" × 42" strips to make binding and bind to finish (see "French Binding" on page 16).

🐰 SUGAR BUNNY HEADBOARD

Finished Headboard Size: 27" × 20"

Materials: (42"-wide fabric)

⅞ yd. pink print or solid flannel for background
¼ yd. cream subtle print or solid for bunny appliqué*
¼ yd. yellow print for dress appliqué
⅛ yd. blue or green print for shoe and collar appliqués*
Assorted scraps to total ⅛ yd. for dress stars and inner ear appliqués*
⅛ yd. *each* pink, blue, and gold prints or solids for background star appliqués*
½ yd. green print flannel for ruffle
¼ yd. coordinating flannel prints or solids for ties*
30" × 30" square of chenille for backing
30" × 30" square of high-loft, bonded batting
¾ yd. lightweight fusible web
1 skein each of black and pink DMC embroidery floss
2 yds. coordinating ⅛"-wide ribbon

*Or use scraps.

Cutting

From the pink print or solid flannel, cut:
    1 square, 30" × 30", for background
From the green print flannel, cut:
    4 strips, each 3½" × 42", for ruffle
From the coordinating print or solid flannel, cut:
    5 strips, each 2¼" × 20", for ties

Constructing the Headboard Panel

1. Refer to the general instructions to make a full-size template for the headboard (see "Headboard," step 1, page 20).

2. Center the headboard template on the 30" × 30" light front panel. Trace around the template, remove it, and machine baste ⅛" inside the traced line. Cut on the traced line.

3. Use the pattern pieces on pages 139–140 to trace appliqué pieces A through O. Refer to the instructions for "Fusible-Web Appliqué" on page 10 to prepare, cut, fuse, and stitch the appliqués in place on the background panel. You'll need to cut 1 each of pieces A, C, C reversed, D, E, F, G, Ia, Ib, J, J reversed, K, L, and L reversed; 2 each of B and M; 8 each of N and O; and 13 of H. Refer to the diagram on page 96, the project photo, and the diagram on page 100 for guidance in positioning the pieces.

4. Embroider Sugar Bunny's facial features using 2 strands of floss. Use a satin stitch for the eyes (black) and nose (pink), and an outline stitch (black) for the mouth (see "Embroidery Stitches" on page 12). Refer to the diagram on page 96 and the E pattern piece for guidance.

Finishing the Headboard

1. Use the 2¼"-wide strips to construct 5 ties (see "Ties" on page 18).
2. Use the 3½" × 42" strips to construct a single long ruffle (see "Ruffles" on page 18).
3. Refer to the general instructions to add the ruffle and ties and to finish the headboard (see "Headboard" on page 20). Notice that the ruffle runs along only the top curved edge of the headboard. Position the ties as shown.
4. Quilt as desired (see "Quilting" on page 16).
5. Tack the midpoint of a 6" length of ribbon in the center of each star and tie in a bow.

SUGAR BUNNY VALANCE

Finished Valance Size: 57" × 13"
Finished Block Size: 6"

Materials: (42"-wide fabric)

⅛ yd. *each* of light, medium, and dark print flannels in blue *and* green for pieced blocks*
1⅝ yds. pink subtle print flannel for setting triangles (A), top and side borders, and lining
¼ yd. yellow print flannel for bottom border
⅝ yd. blue print flannel for header
⅛ yd. each of yellow, blue, green, and pink prints and/or solids for star appliqués**
Assorted flannel scraps to total ½ yd. for ties
¼ yd. lightweight fusible web
1¼ yds. total of coordinating pink, blue, and/or green ⅛"-wide ribbon

*You should have a light, medium, and dark in each color. Use a total of 6 fabrics.
**Or use scraps.

Cutting

From *each* of the 6 blue and green flannels, cut:
    1 strip, 1½" × 42", for pieced blocks
From the pink print flannel, cut:
    2 strips, each 13½" × 42", for lining
    12 squares, each 5¼" × 5¼", for setting triangles (A)
    2 strips, each 3½" × 9", for side border
    2 strips, each 3" × 42", for top border
From the yellow print flannel, cut:
    2 strips, each 2½" × 42", for bottom border
From the blue print flannel, cut:
    3 strips, each 5" × 42", for header
From the assorted flannel scraps, cut:
    9 strips *total*, each 2¼" × 20", for ties

Assembling the Valance Panel

1. Arrange a light, medium, and dark 1½"-wide blue flannel strip to form a 3-strip set, placing the light strip in the center. With right sides together, pin and sew the strip set, pressing the seams in one direction.

2. Repeat step 1 to arrange and sew one 3-strip set with the 1½"-wide green strips.

3. Measure the width of each strip set, including the seam allowance. (It should be 3½".) Cut each strip set into 3½" segments for a total of 12 segments in each color.

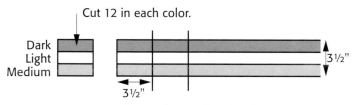

Cut 12 in each color.

Dark
Light
Medium

3½"

3½"

Make 1 strip set of each color.

4. Sew 4 same-color segments together to make a block, rotating the segments as shown. The dark strips should appear in the center of the block to create a pinwheel effect. You'll have a total of 6 blocks, 3 of each color.

Make 3 in each color.

5. Cut each of the 5¼" pink squares on the diagonal in one direction to make a total of 24 setting triangles, 2 from each square. Label these A.

6. Fold each A triangle in half to find the midpoint of its long diagonal side; finger-press to mark. With right sides together, pin an A triangle to opposite sides of each block, matching the triangle midpoint with the block's center seam. Press the seams toward the triangles, then repeat to add a triangle to each of the 2 remaining sides of each block.

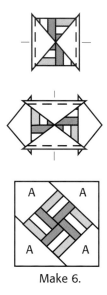

Make 6.

7. Arrange the blocks in a single horizontal row, alternating the colors. Pin and sew the blocks, finishing the row with a 3½" × 9" pink side border strip on each end. Refer to the diagram in step 10 on page 103 as needed.

8. Sew the 2½" × 42" yellow print strips together end to end and cut to make a 2½" × 57½" bottom border strip. Repeat to piece and cut the 3" × 42" pink top border strips and the 13½" × 42" pink lining strips. In the same manner, piece the three 5" × 42" blue header strips and cut 2 strips, each 5" × 57½". Set the lining and header strips aside for now.

9. With right sides together and long raw edges aligned, pin and sew the 3"-wide pink border strip to the top edge of the pieced panel. Press the seams toward the border. Repeat to sew the 2½"-wide yellow border strip to the bottom edge of the panel.

10. Repeat the process described in step 9 to pin, sew, and press 1 blue header strip to the top edge of the pink border strip as shown in the diagram.

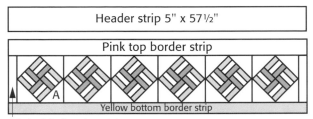

Pink side border strip

11. With right sides together, pin and sew the remaining 5" × 57½" blue header strip to the top long edge of the 13½" × 57½" lining strip.

Lining and Finishing the Valance

1. Use the lining strip to line the valance (see "Valance Lining and Finishing" on page 23).
2. Topstitch with a ¼"-wide seam allowance all around the perimeter of the valance.

3. Use the pattern pieces on page 139 to trace appliqué pieces N and O. Refer to the instructions for "Fusible-Web Appliqué" on page 10 to prepare, cut, fuse, and stitch the appliqués in place on the *back* side of the valance header. If you prefer, you may hand appliqué the star motifs (see "Hand Appliqué" on page 11). You'll need to cut 8 each of N and O. The stars should be evenly spaced along the top edge of the lining, just inside the topstitching. Refer to the project photo on page 101 and the diagram below for guidance in placing the appliqués.

4. Use the 2¼"-wide strips to construct 9 ties (see "Ties" on page 18).

5. Evenly space the 9 ties along the long seam line where the lining and the header meet on the back side of the valance. Pin the ties to secure them, then machine stitch each in place with an **X**. Knot the ends or trim them with pinking shears to finish.

6. Fold the lining header to the front side of the valance along the seam line.

7. Tack the midpoint of a 6" length of ⅛"-wide ribbon at the left and right corners of each pieced block; tie in a bow.

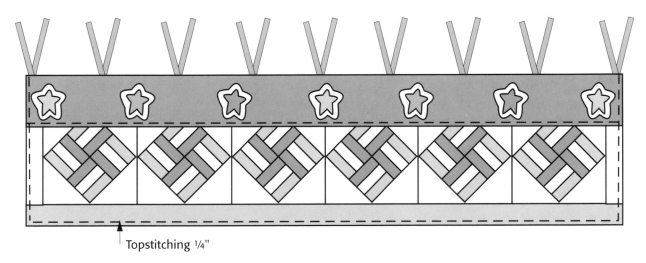

Topstitching ¼"

 ## SUGAR BUNNY DUST RUFFLE

Finished Mattress Base: 27" × 52"
Finished Drop: 19"

Materials: (42"-wide fabric)

1⅝ yds. muslin or a flat crib sheet for mattress base

14½" × 252" green chenille for ruffle

⅜ yd. pink subtle print or solid flannel for accent border

1¾ yds. blue print flannel for bottom border

Cutting

Note: Adjust cutting instructions as needed to match crib measurements (see "Dust Ruffle" on page 22). Seam allowances are ¼" wide.

From the muslin or flat crib sheet, cut:
    1 panel, 28" × 53", for mattress base
From the pink print or solid flannel, cut:
    6 strips, each 1½" × 42", for accent border
From the blue print flannel, cut:
    6 strips, each 9" × 42", for bottom border

Constructing the Dust Ruffle

1. Refer to "Dust Ruffle," steps 1–2, on page 22, to prepare the side, head, and foot ruffle strips from the green chenille, pink accent border, and blue print strips.

2. With wrong sides together, align one long raw edge of each pink accent strip to a blue print border strip of matching length. Sew with a ¼" seam allowance.

3. With wrong sides together, fold the stitched strip in half, matching the long raw edges. Press.

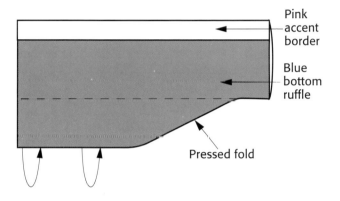

Pink accent border

Blue bottom ruffle

Pressed fold

4. Refer to "Dust Ruffle," steps 3–8, on pages 22–23 to complete the dust ruffle.

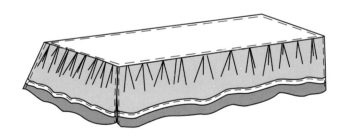

SUGAR BUNNY CRIB QUILT

Finished Quilt Size: 44" × 56"
Finished Block Size: 6"

Materials: (42"-wide fabric)

⅜ yd. *each* of light, medium, and dark print flannels in blues, greens, and pinks*

⅔ yd. yellow subtle print or solid flannel for accent border and binding

⅝ yd. medium green print flannel for outer border**

3 yds. flannel for backing

Crib-size batting (45" × 60")

*You should have a light, medium, and dark in each color. Use a total of 9 fabrics.
**You may use the same medium green print used for the blocks.

Cutting

From *each* of the light, medium, and dark flannels, cut:
    6 strips, each 1½" × 42", for pieced blocks
From the yellow flannel, cut:
    5 strips, each 2½" × 42", for binding
    3 strips, each 1½" × 42", for side accent border
    2 strips, each 1½" × 38½", for top and bottom accent border
From the medium green flannel, cut:
    5 strips, each 3½" × 42", for outer border
From the backing fabric, cut and piece:
    1 panel, 50" × 62" (see "Choosing Batting and Backing" on page 14)

Assembling the Quilt Top

1. Arrange a dark, light, and medium 1½"-wide blue flannel strip to form a 3-strip set, placing the light strip in the center. With right sides together, pin and sew the strip set, pressing

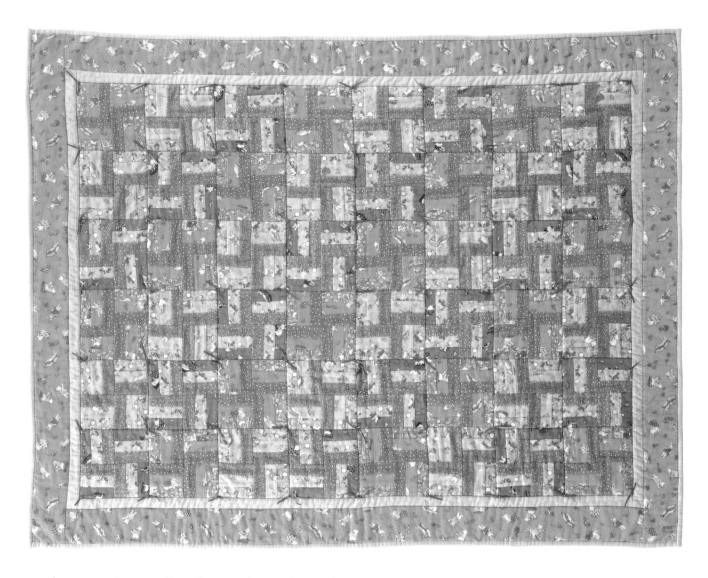

the seams in one direction. Make 6 identical blue strip sets.

2. Repeat step 1 to arrange and sew 6 identical 3-strip sets with the 1½"-wide pink strips, then the 1½"-wide green strips.

3. Measure the width of each strip set, including the seam allowance. (It should be 3½".) Cut each strip set into 3½" segments for a total of 64 segments in each color.

4. Sew 4 same-color segments together to make a block, rotating the segments as shown. The dark strips should appear in the center of the block to create a pinwheel effect. You'll have a total of 48 blocks, 16 of each color.

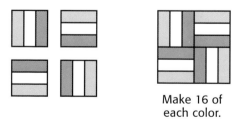

Make 16 of each color.

Cut 64 in each color.

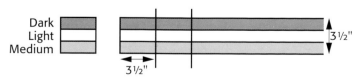

Make 6 strip sets in each color.

5. Arrange the blocks in 8 horizontal rows of 6 blocks each. Begin the first row with a blue block, then a pink, a green, and repeat. Begin the second row with a green, a blue, a pink, and repeat. Begin the third row with a pink, a green, a blue, and repeat. For the fourth row, begin the sequence again, and continue until all of the blocks have been placed. Refer to the quilt photo on page 106 for additional guidance.

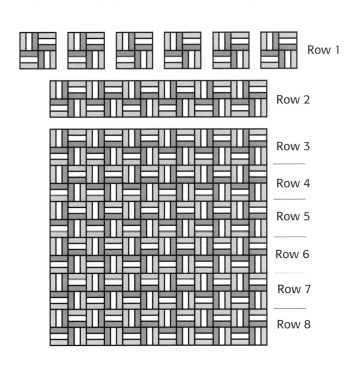

Row 1

Row 2

Row 3

Row 4

Row 5

Row 6

Row 7

Row 8

6. Pin and sew the blocks into rows. Press the joining seams in opposing directions (see "Machine Piecing" on page 8). With right sides together and long raw edges aligned, pin the rows together, sew, and press.

7. Sew the three 1½" × 42" side accent border strips together end to end to make a single long strip. Cut this strip into 2 segments, each 1½" × 48½", for the side accent borders. With right sides together and long raw edges aligned, pin and sew a 1½" × 48½" side accent border strip to each long side of the pieced center. Repeat to add 1½" × 38½" top and bottom accent border strips to the top and bottom edges of the quilt.

8. Sew the five 3½" × 42" green border strips together end to end to make a single long strip. Cut this strip into 2 segments, each 3½" × 50½", for the side outer borders, and 2 segments, each 3½" × 44½", for the top and bottom outer borders. Repeat the process described in step 7 to add the side, then the top and bottom outer border strips to the quilt.

Finishing the Quilt

1. Layer the backing, batting, and quilt top for basting and baste the 3 layers (see "Assembling the Layers" on page 15).

2. Quilt as desired (see "Quilting" on page 16).

3. Use the 2½" × 42" strips to make binding and bind to finish (see "French Binding" on page 16).

Little Sailor's Dream

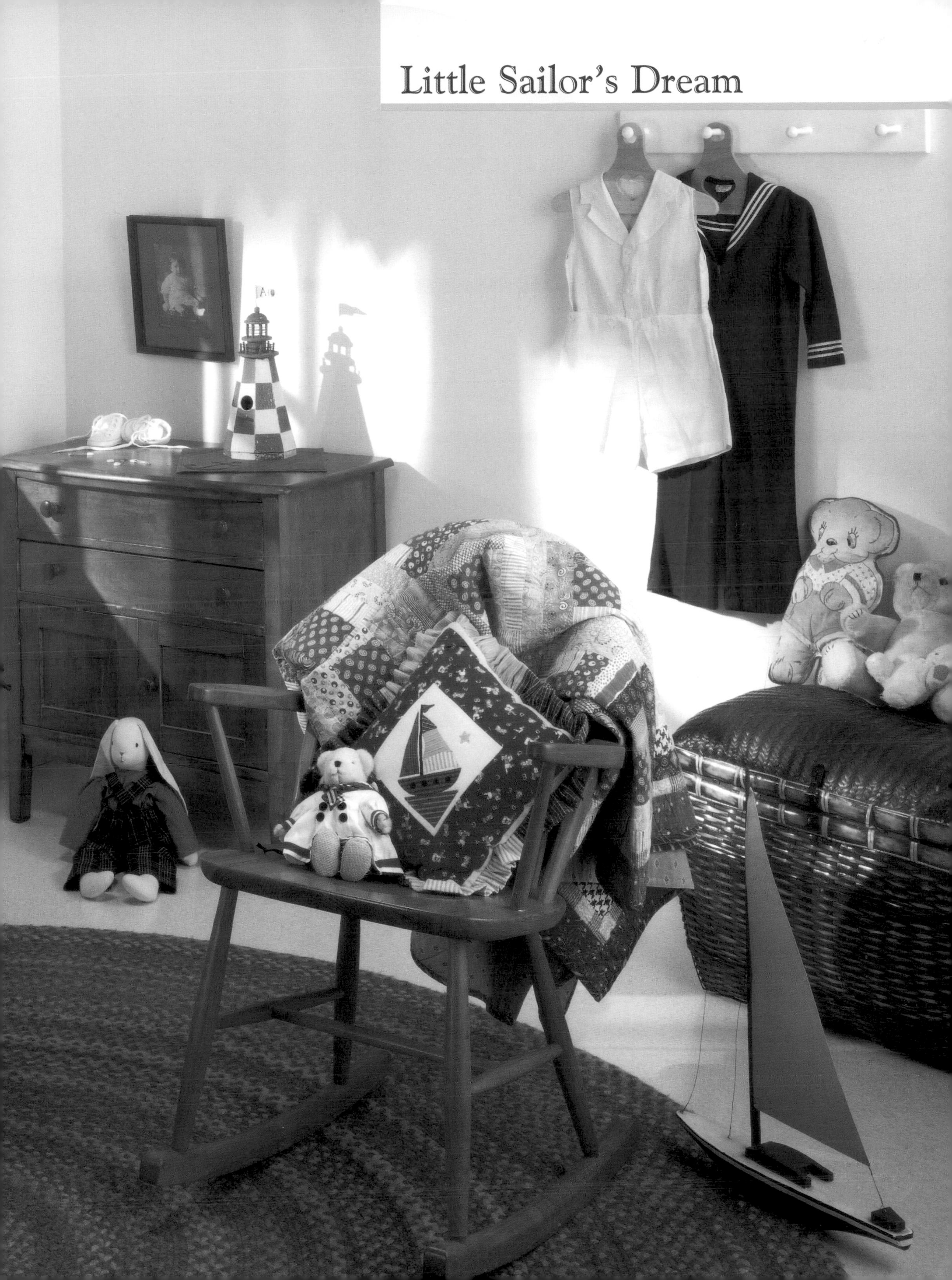

Little Sailor's Dream

Your little one will sail away to dreamland under this combination pieced and solid-block flannel quilt in a snappy red, white, and blue color scheme. The window treatment is easy as a breeze with its red and blue flannel squares, sailboats, and anchor appliqués. The colorful matching headboard and bumper pad are sure to hold his attention for a long time, while the flannel dust ruffle, tossed with appliquéd gold stars, is just right for the little "Captain" of your ship.

LITTLE SAILOR'S DREAM BUMPER PAD

Finished Bumper Pad Size: 137½" × 11½"
Finished Block Size: 9"

Materials: (42"-wide fabric)

½ yd. white or very light print or solid flannel for sailboat background

½ yd. red stripe flannel for anchor background

3/8 yd. blue stripe flannel for water

1/8 yd. *each* of yellow, blue, red, and black stripe and solid flannels for appliqués*

½ yd. navy blue solid flannel for border

5/8 yd. red solid flannel for piping cover

37/8 yds. of 1"-diameter piping

11/3 yds. flannel for backing

½ yd. coordinating print flannel for ties

12" × 138" panel of high-loft, bonded batting**

¾ yd. lightweight fusible web

*Or use scraps.
**Batting may be pieced.

Cutting

From the light print or solid flannel, cut:
   2 strips, each 7" × 42", for sailboat background
From the red stripe flannel, cut:
   2 strips, each 7" × 42", for anchor background
From the blue stripe flannel, cut:
   4 strips, each 3" × 42", for water
From the navy blue solid flannel, cut:
   8 strips, each 1¾" × 42", for border
From the red solid flannel, cut:
   5 strips, each 3" × 42", for piping cover
From the backing flannel, cut:
   4 strips, each 12" × 42"
From the coordinating print flannel, cut:
   12 strips, each 2¼" × 20", for ties

Assembling the Bumper Pad Panel

You will need 8 Anchor blocks and 7 Sailboat blocks for the Little Sailor's Dream Bumper Pad.

1. With right sides together and long raw edges aligned, pin and sew a 7" × 42" light background strip to a 3" × 42" blue water strip. Press toward the blue fabric. The strip set will measure 9½". Repeat to make another identical strip set.

2. Repeat the process described in step 1, this time using the red and blue stripe flannels to make 2 strip sets.

3. Crosscut each of the strip sets into 9½" segments. Cut 7 light/blue segments and 8 red/blue segments.

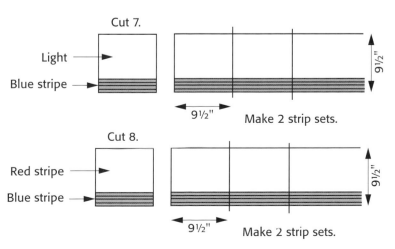

Cut 7.

Light →

Blue stripe →

9½"

9½"

Make 2 strip sets.

Cut 8.

Red stripe →

Blue stripe →

9½"

9½"

Make 2 strip sets.

4. Use the pattern pieces on pages 141–142 to trace appliqué pieces B through J and L. Refer to the instructions for "Fusible-Web Appliqué" on page 10 to prepare, cut, fuse, and stitch the appliqués in place on the pieced background blocks. If you prefer, you may hand appliqué the motifs (see "Hand Appliqué" on page 11). You'll need to cut 7 each of B, C, D, E, F, G, H, and I; 28 J; and 8 L. Refer to the diagrams on page 112 to position pieces B through J on the 7 pieced light background blocks. Center the anchor (L) at

the "waterline" on the 8 pieced red blocks. Refer to the project photo on page 111 for additional guidance in positioning the appliqués.

5. Sew the 1¾" × 42" navy blue flannel strips end to end to make a single long strip. From this strip, cut two 1¾" × 9½" strips for the side border, and two 1¾" × 138" strips for the top and bottom border.

6. Arrange the 15 blocks in a horizontal row as shown in the first diagram below. Begin with an Anchor block, then alternate blocks. Press as desired.

7. With right sides together, pin and sew a 1¾" × 9½" border strip to each short end of the pieced panel. Press toward the border. Repeat to pin and sew 1¾" × 138" top and bottom border strips to the top and bottom of the pieced panel.

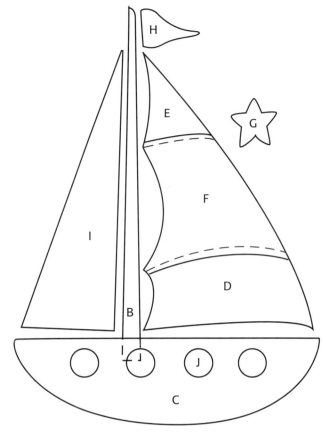

Piping

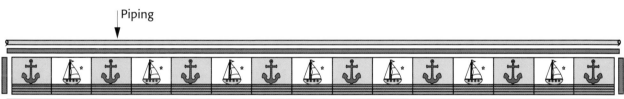

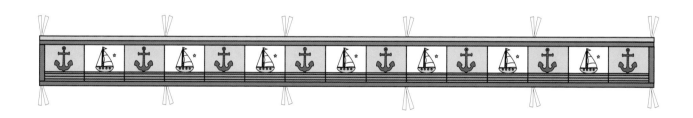

Finishing the Bumper Pad

1. Use the 3" × 42" red flannel strips to construct a single long strip. Cut the strip 138" long and use it to construct piping (see "Piping" on page 19).

2. Use the 2¼"-wide strips to construct 12 ties (see "Ties" on page 18).

3. Refer to the general instructions to add the piping and ties and to finish the bumper pad (see "Bumper Pad" on page 20). Notice in the last diagram on page 112 that the piping runs along only the top edge of the bumper pad, while the ties are along the top and bottom edges.

4. Quilt as desired (see "Quilting" on page 16). You might quilt beside the seam allowances (in-the-ditch) between the blocks and add any other motifs you wish.

 LITTLE SAILOR'S DREAM HEADBOARD

Finished Headboard Size: 27" × 20"
Finished Block Size: 9"

Materials: (42"-wide fabric)

³⁄₈ yd. white or very light print or solid for sailboat background

7" × 9½" rectangle of red stripe flannel for anchor background

³⁄₈ yd. blue stripe flannel for water

½ yd. red print flannel for plain blocks and bottom border

Assorted small scraps of blue, yellow, red, and black solids and stripes for appliqués

½ yd. navy blue flannel for piping cover and ties

⁷⁄₈ yd. flannel for backing

30" × 30" square of high-loft, bonded batting

⅓ yd. lightweight fusible web

1²⁄₃ yds. of 1"-diameter piping

Cutting

From the light print or solid flannel, cut:
    1 strip, 7" × 42", for sailboat appliqué background

From the blue stripe flannel, cut:
    1 strip, 3" × 42", for sailboat water
    1 strip, 3" × 9½", for anchor water

From the red print flannel, cut:
    2 squares, each 9½" × 9½", for plain blocks
    1 strip, 3" × 27½", for bottom border

From the navy blue flannel, cut:
    2 strips, each 3" × 42", for piping cover
    5 strips, each 2½" × 20", for ties

From the backing flannel, cut:
    1 square, 30" × 30"

Constructing the Headboard Panel

1. With right sides together and long raw edges aligned, pin and sew the 7" × 42" light background strip to the 3" × 42" blue water strip. Press toward the blue fabric. The strip set will measure 9½". Crosscut the strip set into 9½" segments. Cut 3.

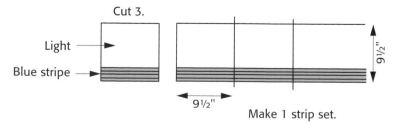

Light →

Blue stripe →

Cut 3.

9½"

9½"

Make 1 strip set.

2. With right sides together and long raw edges aligned, pin and sew the 7" × 9½" red stripe rectangle to the 3" × 9½" blue stripe strip. Press toward the red rectangle.

3. Use the pattern pieces on pages 141–142 to trace appliqué pieces B through J and L. Refer to the instructions for "Fusible-Web Appliqué" on page 10 to prepare, cut, fuse, and stitch the appliqués in place on the pieced background blocks. If you prefer, you may hand appliqué the motifs (see "Hand Appliqué" on page 11). You'll need to cut 3 each of B, C, D, E, F, G, H, and I; 12 J; and

1 L. Refer to the diagrams on page 112 to position pieces B through J on the 3 pieced light background blocks. Center the anchor (L) at the "waterline" on the pieced red block. Refer to the project photo on page 114 and the diagrams at right for additional guidance in positioning the appliqués.

4. Arrange the blocks in 2 horizontal rows. Row 1 alternates a plain block, a Sailboat block, and a plain block. Row 2 alternates a Sailboat block, an Anchor block, and a Sailboat block. Refer to the project photo and the Project Diagram for additional guidance.

5. Pin and sew the blocks into rows, pressing the seams in opposing directions (see "Machine Piecing" on page 8). Pinning carefully to match the seams, sew the rows together and press.

6. With right sides together and long raw edges aligned, sew the 3" × 27½" red print bottom border strip to the bottom edge of the panel.

Finishing the Headboard

1. Refer to "Headboard," steps 1 and 2, on pages 20–21 to make a template for the headboard. Trace, machine baste, and cut the headboard as instructed.

2. Use the 2" × 42" navy blue flannel strips to construct a single long strip. Measure the outside curve of the headboard, cut the strip to this length, and use it to construct piping (see "Piping" on page 19).

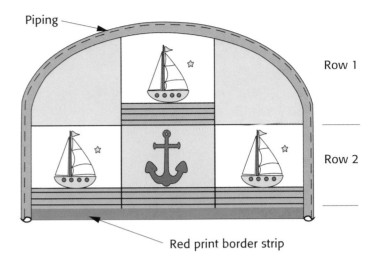

Piping

Row 1

Row 2

Red print border strip

3. Refer to the general instructions to add the piping and ties and to finish the headboard (see "Headboard," steps 5–10, on page 21). Notice that the piping runs along only the curved top edge of the headboard. Position the ties as shown.

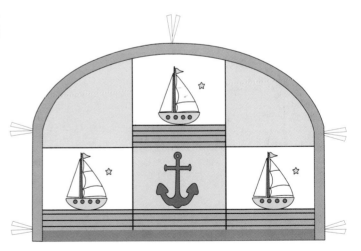

 ## LITTLE SAILOR'S DREAM WINDOW TREATMENT

Fits a window up to 65" wide.

Materials: (42"-wide fabric)

1¼ yds. red stripe flannel for anchor squares

⅞ yd. white or cream flannel for sailboat squares

⅛ yd. *each* of blue, yellow, cream, red, and black solid and stripe flannel for appliqués*

½ yd. lightweight fusible web

*Or use scraps.

Cutting

From the red stripe flannel, cut:

8 squares, each 12½" × 12½", for anchor backgrounds and facings

From the white or cream flannel, cut:

6 squares, each 12½" × 12½", for sailboat backgrounds and facings

Constructing the Window Treatment

1. Use the pattern pieces on pages 141–142 to trace appliqué pieces B through L. Refer to the instructions for "Fusible-Web Appliqué" on page 10 to prepare, cut, fuse, and stitch the appliqués in place. If you prefer, you may hand appliqué the motifs (see "Hand Appliqué" on page 11). You'll need to cut 3 each of B, C, D, E, F, G, H, I, and K; 12 J; and 4 L. Refer to the diagrams below to position pieces B through K on each of the 3 light blocks and an L piece on each of the 4 red stripe blocks. All appliqués should be positioned ¾" from the bottom corner of the square. Refer to the project photo on page 116 for additional guidance in positioning the appliqués.

2. With right sides together, sew matching appliqué and plain blocks together in pairs. Use a ¼"-wide seam allowance, and leave a 4" opening on one side for turning.

3. Trim the seam allowance, clip the corners if necessary, and turn the stitched squares right side out. Press, then slipstitch the openings closed.

4. Topstitch ¼" all around the outside edge of each square.

5. Fold the squares over a decorative rod, overlapping the edges and alternating Anchor and Sailboat blocks.

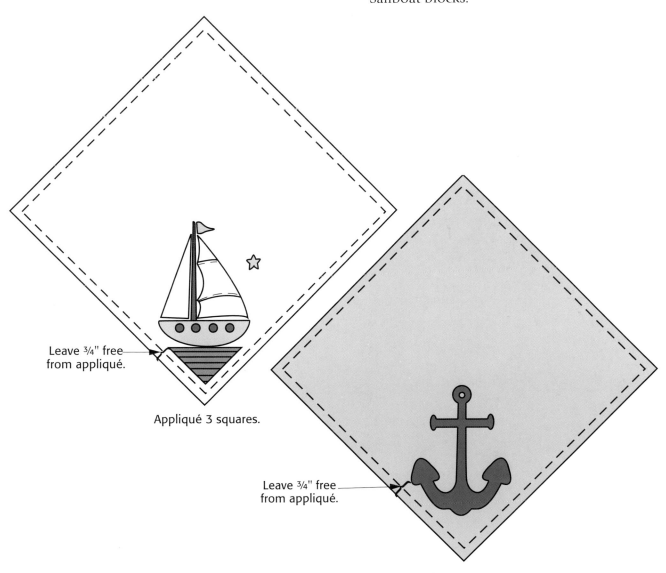

Leave ¾" free from appliqué.

Appliqué 3 squares.

Leave ¾" free from appliqué.

Appliqué 4 squares.

 ## LITTLE SAILOR'S DREAM DUST RUFFLE

Finished Mattress Base: 27" × 52"
Finished Drop: 16"

Materials: (42"-wide fabric)

1⅝ yds. muslin or a flat crib sheet for mattress base
3 yds. blue-and-white check flannel for ruffle
⅝ yd. red solid flannel for piping cover
Yellow scraps to total ⅛ yd. for star appliqués
7⅛ yds. of 1"-diameter piping
¼ yd. lightweight fusible web

Cutting

Note: Adjust cutting instructions as needed to match crib measurements (see "Dust Ruffle" on page 22). Seam allowances are ¼" wide.

From the muslin or flat crib sheet, cut:
    1 panel, 28" × 53", for mattress base
From the blue-and-white check flannel, cut:
    6 strips, each 17" × 42", for ruffle
From the red solid flannel, cut:
    6 strips, each 3" × 42", for piping cover

Constructing the Dust Ruffle

1. Refer to "Dust Ruffle," step 1, on page 22 to prepare the side, head, and foot ruffle strips from the 17" × 42"-long blue-and-white check strips.

2. Repeat to prepare side, head, and foot piping covers from the 3" × 42" red flannel strips. Use these strips to construct piping for each of the ruffle strips (see "Piping" on page 19).

3. With right sides together and raw edges aligned, sew the piping to the bottom edge of the dust ruffle strips.

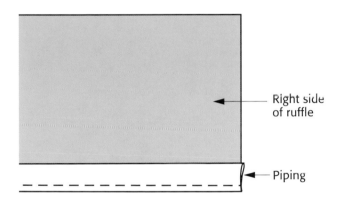

Right side of ruffle

Piping

4. Finish the short ends of the ruffle strips, including the piping, with a double ½" fold and topstitch to secure.

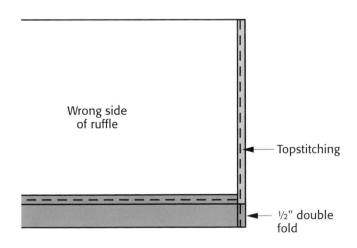

Wrong side of ruffle

Topstitching

½" double fold

5. Use the pattern piece on page 141 to trace appliqué piece A. Refer to the instructions for "Fusible-Web Appliqué" on page 10 to prepare, cut, fuse, and stitch the appliqués in place on the background panel. If you prefer, you can hand appliqué the star motifs (see "Hand Appliqué" on page 11). You'll need to cut 24 star appliqués. "Sprinkle" them evenly around the dust ruffle, placing 8 on each of the side ruffles, and 4 on each of the head and foot ruffles. Refer to the diagram below for guidance in positioning the appliqués.

6. Refer to "Dust Ruffle," steps 2–8, on pages 22–23 to complete the dust ruffle.

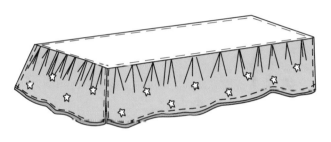

⛵ LITTLE SAILOR'S DREAM LITTLE CRIB QUILT

Finished Quilt Size: 37¾" × 49¼"

Materials: (42"-wide fabric)

¼ yd. *each* of light, medium, and dark print flannels in blue and/or white for pieced blocks*

1 yd. red print flannel for corner triangles and outer border

⅝ yd. white or other very light print or solid flannel for plain blocks

¼ yd. navy blue subtle print or solid flannel for accent border

1½ yds. flannel for backing

½ yd. fabric for binding

Crib-size batting (45" × 60")

*Use a total of 3 fabrics.

Cutting

From *each* of the light and medium blue and/or white print flannels, cut:

    2 strips, each 1¾" × 42", for pieced blocks

From the dark blue print flannel, cut:

    2 strips, each 2" × 42", for pieced blocks

From the red print flannel, cut:

    2 strips, each 4" × 42¾", for side outer border

    2 strips, each 4" × 38¼", for top and bottom outer border

    36 squares, each 3⅞" × 3⅞", for setting triangles

From the white print or solid flannel, cut:

    17 squares, each 6¼" × 6¼", for plain blocks

From the navy blue print or solid flannel, cut:

    2 strips, each 1½" × 40¼", for side accent border

    2 strips, each 1½" × 30¾", for top and bottom accent border

From the backing flannel, cut:

    1 panel, 42" × 53"

From the binding fabric, cut:

    5 strips, each 2½" × 42"

Assembling the Quilt Top

You will need 18 pieced blocks for the Little Sailor's Dream Flannel Quilt. The strip-set block finished 4", but you will be setting it "on-point" with corner triangles. Turning a block on-point can sometimes yield strange measurements. In this case, the block finishes to approximately 5.65", which we will round off to 5¾". Therefore, the cut size of the plain blocks is 6¼".

1. Arrange a 1¾" light and medium flannel strip on either side of a 2" dark flannel strip to form a 3-strip set. With right sides together, pin and sew the strip set, pressing the seams away from the center strip. Make 2 identical strip sets.

2. Measure the width of each strip set, including the seam allowance. (It should be 4½".) Cut each strip set into 4½" segments for a total of 18 segments.

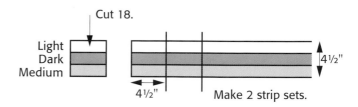

Make 2 strip sets.

3. Cut each of the 3⅞" red print squares on the diagonal in one direction to make a total of 72 setting triangles, 2 from each square.

4. Fold each corner triangle in half to find the midpoint of the long diagonal side and finger-press to mark. Fold each block in half in both directions to find and finger-press its midpoint on all 4 sides. With right sides together, pin a corner triangle to opposite sides of each block, matching the triangle midpoint with the block midpoint. Press the seams toward the triangles, then repeat to add a triangle to the 2 remaining sides of each block.

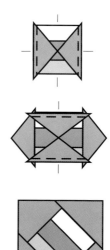

Make 18.

5. Arrange the pieced and plain blocks in 7 horizontal rows of 5 blocks each, alternating pieced and plain blocks. Odd-numbered rows (1, 3, 5, and 7) should begin and end with a pieced block. Even-numbered rows (2, 4, and 6) should begin and end with a plain block as shown.

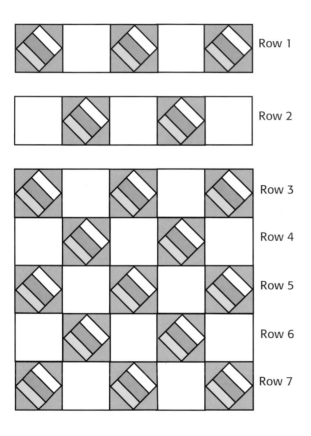

Row 1
Row 2
Row 3
Row 4
Row 5
Row 6
Row 7

6. With right sides together and long raw edges aligned, pin and sew a 1½" × 40¼" side accent border strip to each long side of the quilt top. Press the seams toward the border. Repeat to add 1½" × 30¾" top and bottom accent border strips to the top and bottom edges of the quilt top (see "Adding Borders" on page 13).

7. Repeat the procedure described in step 6 to add a 4" × 42¾" side outer border strip to each side of the quilt top, and 4" × 38¼" top and bottom outer border strips to the top and bottom edges.

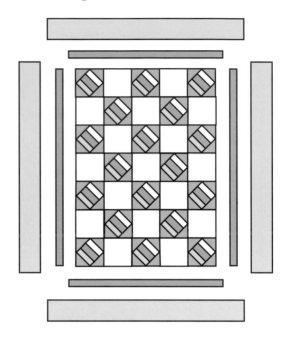

Finishing the Quilt

1. Layer the backing, batting, and quilt top for basting and baste the 3 layers (see "Assembling the Layers" on page 15).
2. Quilt as desired (see "Quilting" on page 16).
3. Use the 2½" × 42" strips to make binding and bind to finish (see "French Binding" on page 17).

 ## LITTLE SAILOR'S DREAM ANCHOR PILLOW

Finished Pillow Size: 12" square

Materials (42"-wide fabric) and Cutting

1 square, 6½" × 6½", white or cream flannel for background

2 strips, each 3½" × 6½", navy blue stripe flannel for side border*

2 strips, each 3½" × 12½", of *same* navy blue stripe flannel for top and bottom border*

*Navy blue stripe flannel totals ¼ yard.

Small yellow and blue scraps for appliqués

2 strips, each 2½" × 42", red solid flannel for piping cover (¼ yd.)

12½" × 12½" flannel square for backing

⅛ yd. lightweight fusible web

1¾ yds. of 1"-diameter piping

Small bag of polyester fiberfill or 12" pillow form

Constructing the Pillow

1. With rights sides together and raw edges aligned, sew 3½" × 6½" side border strips to 2 opposite sides of the light square. Press toward the border. Repeat to sew 3½" × 12½"

top and bottom border strips to the remaining sides of the square.

2. Use the pattern pieces on pages 141–142 to trace appliqué pieces A and L. Refer to the instructions for "Fusible-Web Appliqué" on page 10 to prepare, cut, fuse, and stitch the appliqués in place on the light background block (anchor) and in the 4 corners of the border (stars). If you prefer, you may hand appliqué the motifs (see "Hand Appliqué" on page 11). Refer to the project photo on page 123 and the diagram below for guidance in positioning the appliqués.

3. Join the 2½" × 42" red flannel strips to construct a single long strip and use it to construct piping (see "Piping" on page 19).

4. Refer to "Pillow Finishing" on page 23 to complete the project.

LITTLE SAILOR'S DREAM FLANNEL SAILBOAT PILLOW

Finished Pillow Size: 13" × 13" (plus ruffle)

Materials (42"-wide fabric) and Cutting

1 square, 6½" × 6½", white or cream flannel for background

2 strips, each 3½" × 6½", red print flannel for side border*

2 strips, each 3½" × 12½", of *same* red print flannel for top and bottom border*

2 strips, each 1" × 12½", yellow flannel for side accent border**

2 strips, each 1" × 13½", of *same* yellow flannel for top and bottom accent border**

Assorted scraps of blue, red, black, cream, and yellow solid and stripe flannels for appliqués

4½"-wide strips of 4 different color flannels to total 104" for ruffle

1 square, 13½" × 13½", for backing

⅛ yd. lightweight fusible web

Small bag of polyester fiberfill

*Red print flannel totals ¼ yard.

**Yellow flannel totals ⅛ yard.

Constructing the Pillow

1. With rights sides together and raw edges aligned, sew 3½" × 6½" side border strips to 2 opposite sides of the light square. Press toward the border. Repeat to sew 3½" × 12½" top and bottom border strips to the remaining sides of the square.

2. Repeat step 1 to sew 1" × 12½" side accent border strips to 2 sides of the block, and 1" × 13½" accent border strips to the top and bottom edges of the block.

3. Use the pattern pieces on pages 141–142 to trace appliqué pieces B through K. Refer to the instructions for "Fusible-Web Appliqué" on page 10 to prepare, cut, fuse, and stitch the appliqués in place on the pieced background blocks. If you prefer, you may hand appliqué the motifs (see "Hand Appliqué" on page 11). You'll need to cut 1 each of B, C, D, E, F, G, H, I, and K; and 4 J. Refer to the diagrams on page 112 to position pieces B through K on the light background block. Refer to the project photo above for additional guidance in positioning the appliqués.

4. Use the 4½"-wide strips to piece a single scrappy strip 104" long and use it to construct a ruffle (see "Ruffles" on page 18).

5. Refer to "Pillow Finishing" on page 23 to complete the project.

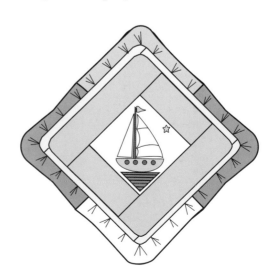

Special Projects

Here are some additional projects you might like to try!

EMBROIDERED BIBS

A quick, easy gift idea! We purchased Battenburg lace–trimmed baby bibs. Referring to the embroidery guides, enlarge and trace the pattern of your choice on the center of the bib. Embroider with two strands of DMC embroidery floss and a stem stitch, unless indicated otherwise (see "Embroidery Stitches" on page 12).

Suggested Thread for Sailboat Bib
#321 Christmas Red (boat)
#676 Old Gold Light (star)
#700 Christmas Green (sail)
#945 Sportsman Flesh (mast)
#824 Blue (water)

Size as needed.

Suggested Thread for Flower Garden Bib
#776 Pink Medium (flower petals)
#368 Pistachio Light (stem, leaves, and grass)
#676 Old Gold Light (flower center; stamen head: French knot, 1 wrap)

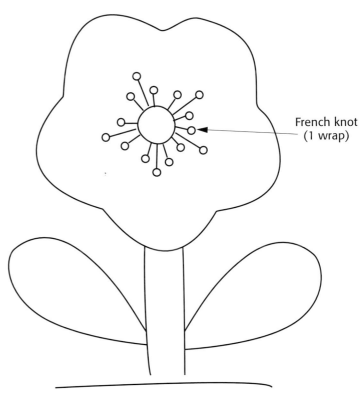

French knot (1 wrap)

Size as needed .

BABY'S APPLIQUÉD SWEATSHIRTS

These darling sweatshirts are decorated with left-over fabrics and appliqué designs borrowed from the various collections in *The Quilted Nursery*. Before you begin, wash and dry the sweatshirt *without fabric softener*. Use lightweight fusible web and a blanket stitch to appliqué the design to the sweatshirt (see "Fusible-Web Appliqué" on page 10 and "Blanket Stitch" on pages 12–13).

Don't just limit this terrific idea to sweatshirts. Toddler-size jackets, shirts, and dresses would be very cute too! Refer to the specific collection for the appliqué patterns and placement guides. The Sugar Bunny sweatshirt is the only design with a special placement diagram.

BABY'S SECRET GARDEN PAINTED FLOOR CLOTH

Finished Floor Cloth Size: 3' × 5'

Floor cloths are an easy project for even the "unrealized" decorative painter. If you have selected one of the other collections in *The Quilted Nursery*, substitute the appropriate pattern and paint colors, then use the basic instructions provided to create a matching floor cloth. If you've never painted before, take a trip to your local craft store; you'll find lots of help and suggestions there. Don't be afraid to try! A painted floor cloth is the perfect finishing touch for your quilted nursery.

Supplies

3' × 5' primed canvas floor cloth
Yardstick
9" paper plate for scalloped border template
Natural sea sponge
Painter's tape, drafting tape, or Scotch Magic Tape
Liner #10/0 brush
1"-wide polyfoam brush for base coating
Large, flat #14 brush
Soft paper towels
Water-soluble tracing paper
Clear acrylic matte sealer
A non-carnauba paste wax, such as Johnson's
Paints:
Delta Ceramcoat Acrylic Colors: #2016 Lavender Lace, #2133 Cape Cod Blue, #2401 Light Ivory, #2445 Green Sea
DecoAmericana: #DA038 Wedgewood Blue, #DA007 Moon Yellow
FolkArt: #753 Rose Chiffon

Preparing the Floor Cloth

1. Measure and outline the borders as follows:
   Outside border: 1" wide
   Middle border: 3" wide
   Inside border: 1½" wide
2. 3" Scalloped Border: Referring to the project photo on page 129 and the diagram below, draw a 3" scalloped border. Half of a paper plate works well as a template. Outline the inside of the scalloped border with small pieces of Scotch Magic Tape or painter's tape. Be sure tape is sealed well to prevent bleed-through. Do this by pressing the edge of tape with your thumbnail or an eraser.

Tip

Tape off areas where you don't want paint to overlap for a neat, finished project.

Painting the Floor Cloth

1. Sponge-paint the middle panel of the floor cloth with Lavender Lace. Let the paint dry.
2. Tape off the outside straight edge of the scalloped border. Sponge-paint inside the scalloped border with Green Sea. Let the paint dry and remove tape from the scalloped border.
3. Apply a base coat to the 1½" border with Wedgewood Blue.
4. Apply a base coat to the 3" border with Lavender Lace and let the paint dry. Section border into 1" squares. Paint a plaid with Cape Cod Blue, Rose Chiffon, and Light Ivory. Refer to the project photo for design suggestions.
5. Apply a base coat to the 1" border with Rose Chiffon.
6. Refer to the project photo for placement suggestions and trace flowers on the floor cloth.
7. Apply a base coat to alternate blossoms with Rose Chiffon and Moon Yellow. Apply the opposite color as the base coat for the blossom centers. Dot all centers with Light Ivory, using a stylus or brush handle.
8. Apply a base coat to the leaves and stems with Green Sea. Paint a plaid using Rose Chiffon, Moon Yellow, and Cape Cod Blue. See photo for design suggestions.

Finishing the Floor Cloth

1. Let the floor cloth dry for 24 hours.
2. Apply 2 to 3 coats of clear acrylic matte sealer. Let the floor cloth dry thoroughly between coats.
3. When dry, apply a non-carnauba paste wax with a soft cloth for added protection and easy cleaning.

Resources

Chenille

Wimpole Street Creations chenille can often be found at your local crafts store. If not, contact:
Barrett House
PO Box 540585
North Salt Lake, UT 54054-0585
Phone: (801) 299-0700

Batting

Warm & Natural needlepunch cotton batting
The Warm Company
954 East Union Street
Seattle, WA 98122
Phone: (800) 234-WARM or (206) 320-9276
Fax: (206) 320-0974
www.warmcompany.com

Fusible web

I use both *Steam-A-Seam 2* and *HeatnBond Lite*. It's a matter of individual preference. *PEELnSTICK* is a double-sided adhesive.

Steam-A-Seam 2
The Warm Company
954 East Union Street
Seattle, WA 98122
Phone: (800) 234-WARM or (206) 320-9276
Fax: (206) 320-0974
www.warmcompany.com

HeatnBond Lite and *PEELnSTICK*
Therm O Web
770 Glenn Avenue
Wheeling, IL 60090
Phone: (800) 323-0799
Fax: (847) 520-0025

Embroidery floss

DMC embroidery floss
The DMC Corporation
10 Port Kearny
South Kearny, NJ 07032
Phone: (201) 589-0606
Fax: (201) 589-8931

Floor cloth

Kreative Kanvas
Foss Manufacturing Co.
380 Lafayette Road
Hampton, NH 03843
Phone: (800) 292-7900
Fax: (603) 929-6180
www.kuninfelt.com

Acrylic paint

We use three brands of acrylic paints, and all are generally available in local craft stores. However, the source of supply is an excellent reference point for specific questions or problems.

Delta Ceramcoat
Delta Technical Coatings, Inc.
2550 Pellissier Place
Whittier, CA 90601
Phone: (213) 686-0678
Fax: (310) 695-5157

FolkArt
Plaid Enterprises
1649 International Ct.
Norcross GA 30093
Phone: (770) 923-8200
Fax: (770) 806-6930

American DecoArt
Ceramichrome, Inc.
PO Box 386
Stanford, KY 40484
Phone: (800) 477-8478
Fax: (606) 365-9739
www.decoart.com

Fiberfill for pillows

Morning Glory Products/Clusterfil
Carpenter Co.
302 Highland Drive
Taylor, TX 76574

About the Author

Leslie Beck

Leslie grew up in a creative, artistic family. Her grandfather, a cabinet maker in Norway, designed and handcrafted furniture. Her father enjoyed drawing, while her mother created and sold art to department stores. Growing up, Leslie and her siblings always had paper, pencils, pens, crayons, and paste along with a healthy, artistic imagination.

Leslie formed Fiber Mosaics, her graphics and design company, in 1985. The company name reflects her love and talent for combining colors, shapes, and textures. Today, Fiber Mosaics by Leslie Beck is credited with more than 200 quilt patterns and booklets. In addition, Leslie designs for V.I.P. Fabrics, Simplicity Pattern Co., Bernina Embroidery Cards, Plaid Decorative Painting and Crafts, Imperial Wallpaper Company, Barth & Dreyfuss Kitchen Textiles, Sakura Dinnerware, The Rug Barn Woven Throws and Pillows, and Evergreen Flags.

Patterns

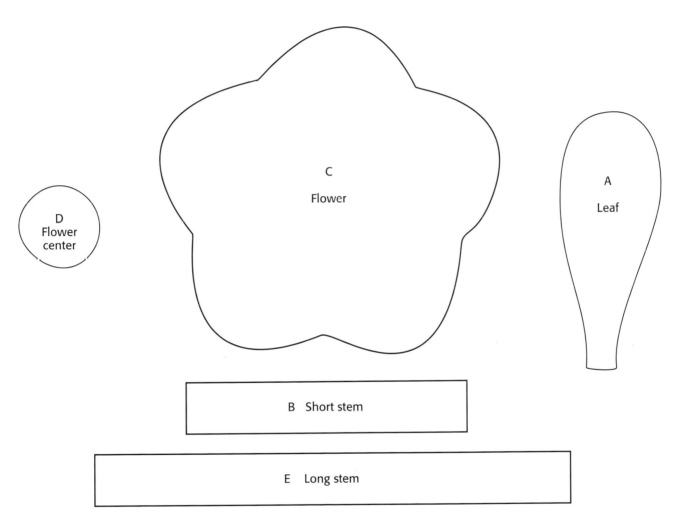

D
Flower
center

C
Flower

A
Leaf

B   Short stem

E   Long stem

Baby's Secret Garden Collecton
Full-size patterns

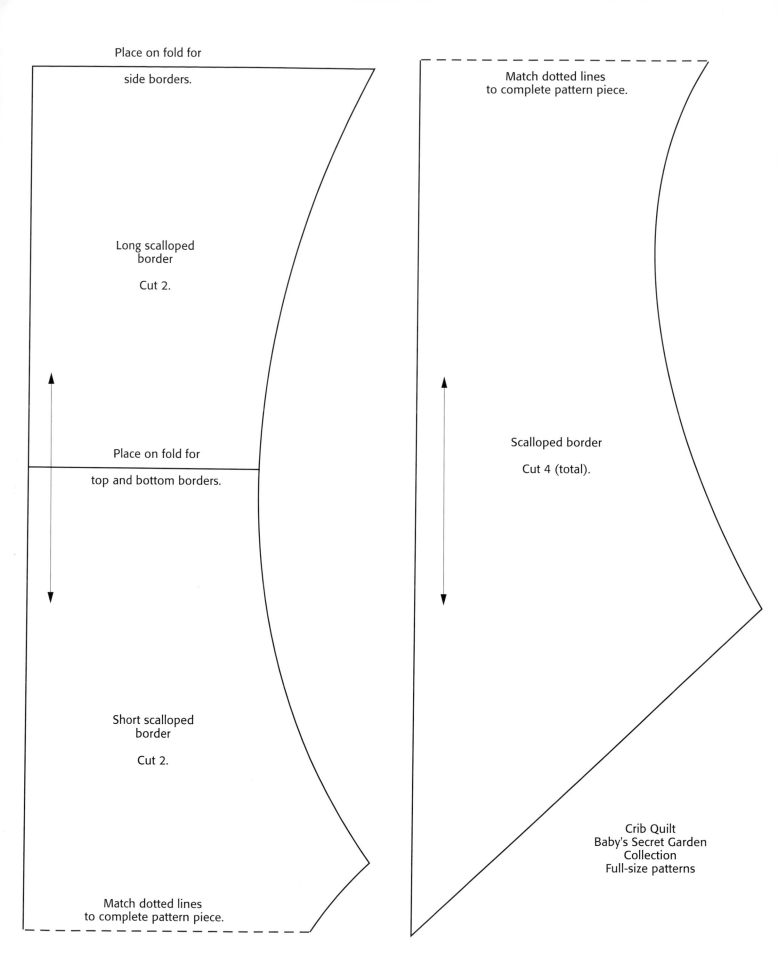

Place on fold for
side borders.

Long scalloped
border

Cut 2.

Place on fold for

top and bottom borders.

Short scalloped
border

Cut 2.

Match dotted lines
to complete pattern piece.

Match dotted lines
to complete pattern piece.

Scalloped border

Cut 4 (total).

Crib Quilt
Baby's Secret Garden
Collection
Full-size patterns

Cut 2 fabric pieces.
Cut 2 interfacing pieces.

F

Diaper Stacker
Top Panel (front and back)

Place on fold of fabric.

(includes ⅝" seam allowance

Baby's Secret Garden Collection
Full-size pattern

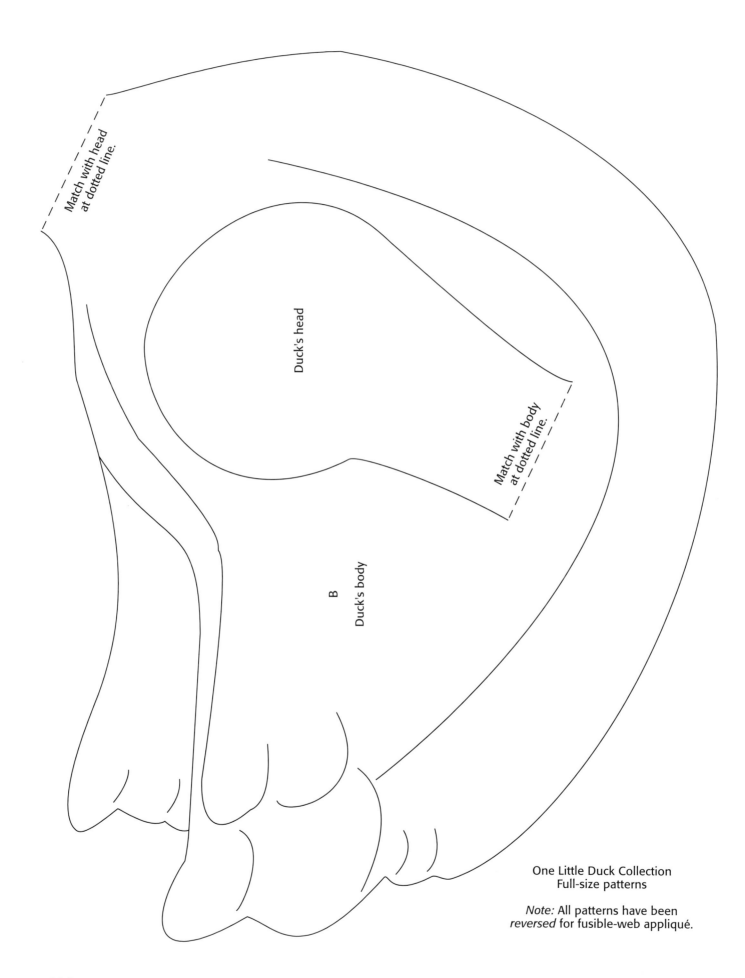

Match with head at dotted line.

Match with body at dotted line.

Duck's head

B
Duck's body

One Little Duck Collection
Full-size patterns

Note: All patterns have been *reversed* for fusible-web appliqué.

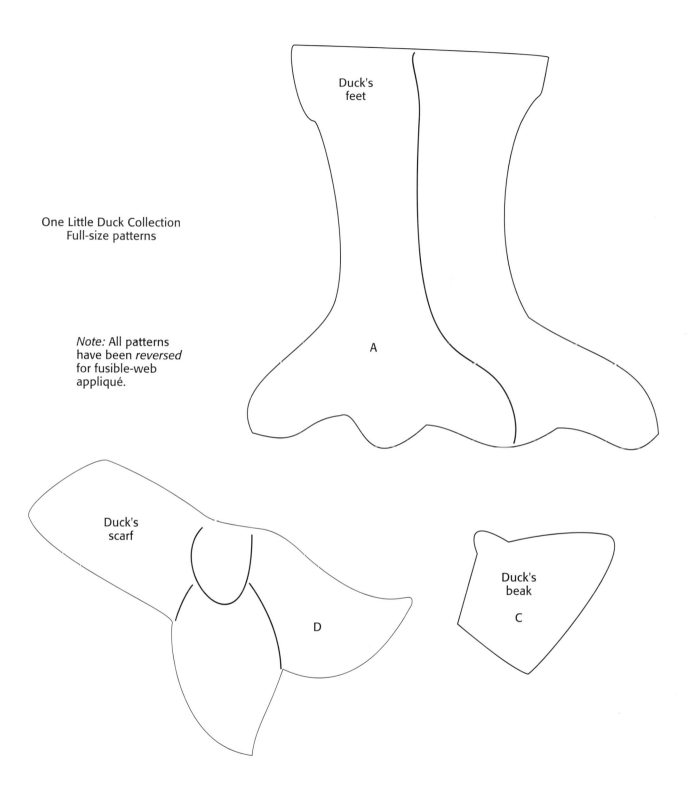

Duck's feet

A

One Little Duck Collection
Full-size patterns

Note: All patterns have been *reversed* for fusible-web appliqué.

Duck's scarf

D

Duck's beak

C

Note: All patterns have been *reversed* for fusible-web appliqué.

One Little Duck Collection
Full-size patterns

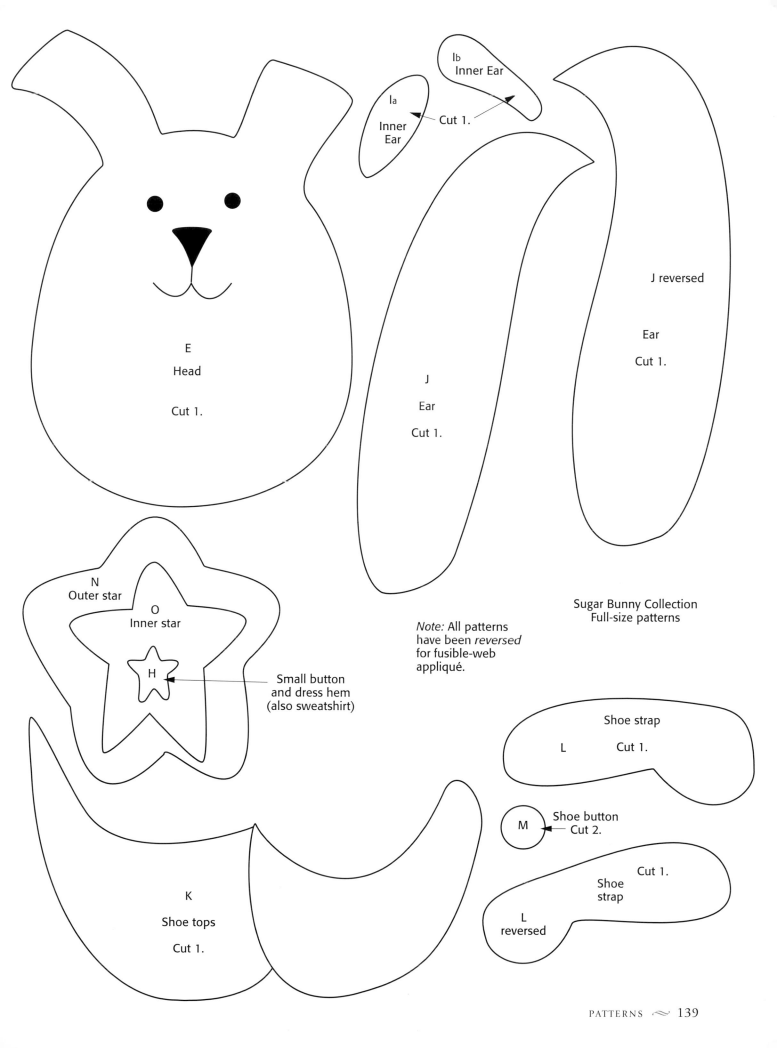

I_b
Inner Ear

I_a
Inner Ear

Cut 1.

E
Head

Cut 1.

J reversed

Ear

Cut 1.

J
Ear
Cut 1.

Sugar Bunny Collection
Full-size patterns

Note: All patterns
have been *reversed*
for fusible-web
appliqué.

N
Outer star

O
Inner star

H

Small button
and dress hem
(also sweatshirt)

Shoe strap

L   Cut 1.

M   Shoe button
Cut 2.

Cut 1.
Shoe
strap

K

Shoe tops

Cut 1.

L
reversed

F   Cut 1.

Collar

B

Hand

Cut 2.

Sugar Bunny
Collection
Full-size patterns

G

Dress button

Cut 1.

C

Arm

Cut 1.

C
reversed

Arm

Cut 1.

Note: All patterns
have been *reversed*
for fusible-web
appliqué.

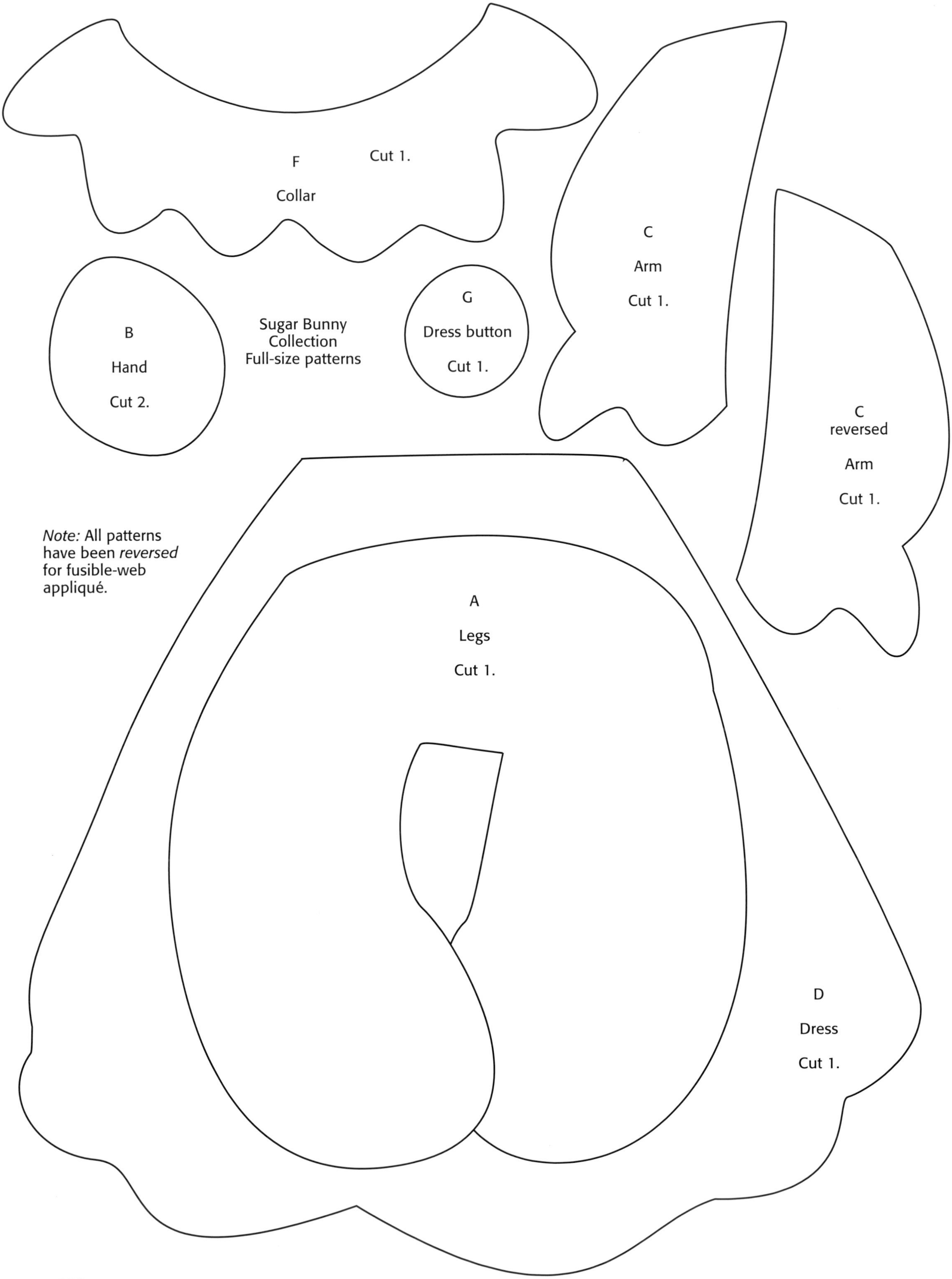

A

Legs

Cut 1.

D

Dress

Cut 1.

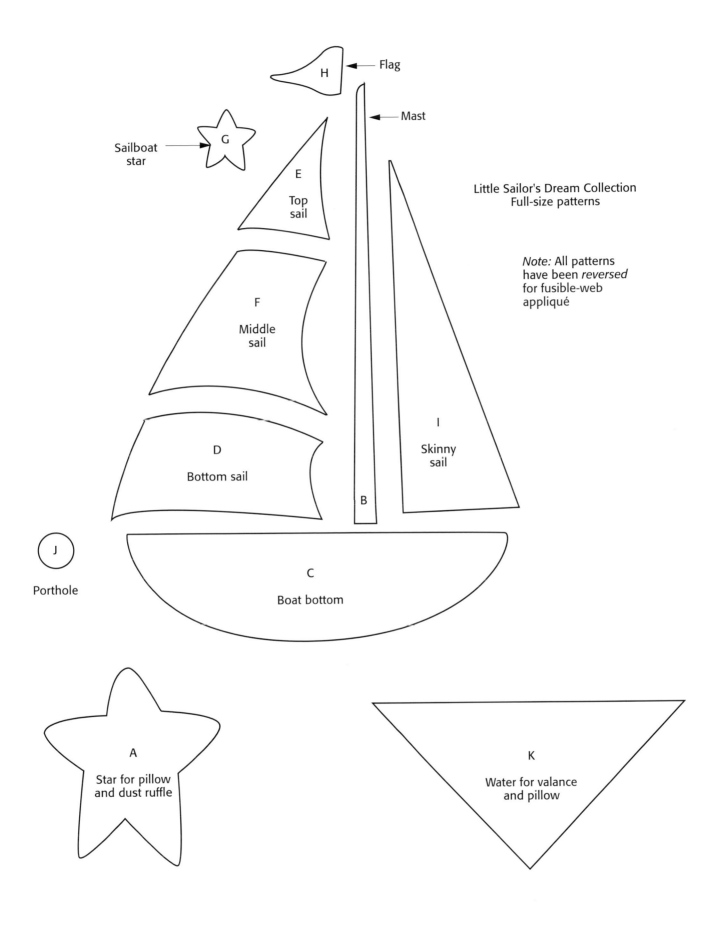

Flag

H

Mast

Sailboat
star

G

E

Top
sail

Little Sailor's Dream Collection
Full-size patterns

Note: All patterns
have been *reversed*
for fusible-web
appliqué

F

Middle
sail

I

Skinny
sail

D

Bottom sail

B

J

Porthole

C

Boat bottom

A

Star for pillow
and dust ruffle

K

Water for valance
and pillow

L

Anchor

Little Sailor's Dream Collection
Full-size pattern

Notes

Books from Martingale & Company

Appliqué
Appliqué in Bloom
Baltimore Bouquets
Basic Quiltmaking Techniques for Hand Appliqué
Basic Quiltmaking Techniques for Machine Appliqué
Coxcomb Quilt
The Easy Art of Appliqué
Folk Art Animals
From a Quilter's Garden
Fun with Sunbonnet Sue
Garden Appliqué
Interlacing Borders
Once Upon a Quilt
Stars in the Garden
Sunbonnet Sue All Through the Year
Welcome to the North Pole

Basic Quiltmaking Techniques
Basic Quiltmaking Techniques for Borders & Bindings
Basic Quiltmaking Techniques for Curved Piecing
Basic Quiltmaking Techniques for Divided Circles
Basic Quiltmaking Techniques for Eight-Pointed Stars
Basic Quiltmaking Techniques for Hand Appliqué
Basic Quiltmaking Techniques for Machine Appliqué
Basic Quiltmaking Techniques for Strip Piecing
Your First Quilt Book (or it should be!)

Crafts
15 Beads
The Art of Handmade Paper and Collage
Christmas Ribbonry
Fabric Mosaics
Folded Fabric Fun
Hand-Stitched Samplers from I Done My Best
The Home Decorator's Stamping Book
Making Memories
A Passion for Ribbonry
Stamp with Style

Design Reference
Color: The Quilter's Guide
Design Essentials: The Quilter's Guide
Design Your Own Quilts
The Nature of Design
QuiltSkills
Surprising Designs from Traditional Quilt Blocks

Foundation/Paper Piecing
Classic Quilts with Precise Foundation Piecing
Crazy but Pieceable
Easy Machine Paper Piecing
Easy Mix & Match Machine Paper Piecing
Easy Paper-Pieced Keepsake Quilts
Easy Paper-Pieced Miniatures
Easy Reversible Vests
Go Wild with Quilts
Go Wild with Quilts—Again!
It's Raining Cats & Dogs
Mariner's Medallion
Paper Piecing the Seasons
A Quilter's Ark
Sewing on the Line
Show Me How to Paper Piece

Home Decorating
Decorate with Quilts & Collections
The Home Decorator's Stamping Book
Living with Little Quilts
Make Room for Quilts
Special-Occasion Table Runners
Stitch & Stencil
Welcome Home: Debbie Mumm
Welcome Home: Kaffe Fassett

Joy of Quilting Series
Borders by Design
The Easy Art of Appliqué
A Fine Finish

Hand-Dyed Fabric Made Easy
Happy Endings
Loving Stitches
Machine Quilting Made Easy
A Perfect Match
Press for Success
Sensational Settings
Shortcuts
The Ultimate Book of Quilt Labels

Knitting
Simply Beautiful Sweaters
Two Sticks and a String
Welcome Home: Kaffe Fassett

Machine Quilting/Sewing
Machine Needlelace
Machine Quilting Made Easy
Machine Quilting with Decorative Threads
Quilting Makes the Quilt
Thread Magic
Threadplay

Miniature/Small Quilts
Celebrate! with Little Quilts
Crazy but Pieceable
Easy Paper-Pieced Miniatures
Fun with Miniature Log Cabin Blocks
Little Quilts All Through the House
Living with Little Quilts
Miniature Baltimore Album Quilts
Small Quilts Made Easy
Small Wonders

Quilting/Finishing Techniques
Borders by Design
The Border Workbook
A Fine Finish
Happy Endings
Interlacing Borders
Loving Stitches
Quilt It!
Quilting Design Sourcebook
Quilting Makes the Quilt
Traditional Quilts with Painless Borders
The Ultimate Book of Quilt Labels

Rotary Cutting/Speed Piecing
101 Fabulous Rotary-Cut Quilts
All-Star Sampler
Around the Block with Judy Hopkins
Bargello Quilts
Basic Quiltmaking Techniques for Strip Piecing
Block by Block
Easy Seasonal Wall Quilts
Easy Star Sampler
Fat Quarter Quilts
The Heirloom Quilt
The Joy of Quilting
More Quilts for Baby
More Strip-Pieced Watercolor Magic
A New Slant on Bargello Quilts
A New Twist on Triangles
Patchwork Pantry
Quilters on the Go
Quilting Up a Storm
Quilts for Baby
Quilts from Aunt Amy
ScrapMania
Simply Scrappy Quilts
Square Dance
Strip-Pieced Watercolor Magic
Stripples Strikes Again!
Strips That Sizzle
Two-Color Quilts

Seasonal Projects
Christmas Ribbonry
Easy Seasonal Wall Quilts

Folded Fabric Fun
Holiday Happenings
Quilted for Christmas
Quilted for Christmas, Book III
Quilted for Christmas, Book IV
A Silk-Ribbon Album
Welcome to the North Pole

Stitchery/Needle Arts
Christmas Ribbonry
Crazy Rags
Hand-Stitched Samplers from I Done My Best
Machine Needlelace
Miniature Baltimore Album Quilts
A Passion for Ribbonry
A Silk-Ribbon Album
Victorian Elegance

Surface Design/Fabric Manipulation
15 Beads
The Art of Handmade Paper and Collage
Complex Cloth
Creative Marbling on Fabric
Dyes & Paints
Hand-Dyed Fabric Made Easy
Jazz It Up

Theme Quilts
The Cat's Meow
Everyday Angels in Extraordinary Quilts
Fabric Collage Quilts
Fabric Mosaics
Folded Fabric Fun
Folk Art Quilts
Honoring the Seasons
It's Raining Cats & Dogs
Life in the Country with Country Threads
Making Memories
More Quilts for Baby
The Nursery Rhyme Quilt
Once Upon a Quilt
Patchwork Pantry
Quilted Landscapes
Quilting Your Memories
Quilts for Baby
Quilts from Nature
Through the Window and Beyond
Two-Color Quilts

Watercolor Quilts
More Strip-Pieced Watercolor Magic
Strip-Pieced Watercolor Magic
Watercolor Impressions
Watercolor Quilts

Wearables
Crazy Rags
Dress Daze
Easy Reversible Vests
Jacket Jazz Encore
Just Like Mommy
Variations in Chenille

Many of these books are available through your local quilt, fabric, craft-supply, or art-supply store. For more information, call, write, fax, or e-mail for our free full-color catalog.

Martingale & Company
PO Box 118
Bothell, WA 98041-0118 USA
1-800-426-3126
International: 1-425-483-3313
24-Hour Fax: 1-425-486-7596
Web site: www.patchwork.com
E-mail: info@martingale-pub.com

3/99